Best-kept Secrets of the Women's Institute

CAKES & BISCUITS

Jill Brand

First published in Great Britain by Simon & Schuster UK Ltd, 2002
A Viacom Company

Simon & Schuster UK Ltd
Africa House
64–78 Kingsway
London
WC2B 6AH

1 3 5 7 9 10 8 6 4 2

Design and typesetting: **Fiona Andreanelli**
Food photography: **Steve Baxter**
Home economist: **Sara Buenfeld**
Stylist for food photography: **Liz Belton**
Printed and bound in China

ISBN 0 74322 111 7

CONTENTS

CAKE MAKING – AN INTRODUCTION

It is thought that cake making probably evolved from early pastry making. Pastry was originally a simple paste of flour and water that protected meat from the direct heat used in cooking; juices and fat dripping from the meat on to the flour-and-water paste helped create the first true pastry.

Early cakes and buns were first a doughy mixture with dried fruit, berries and spices added, often to use up pastry scraps prior to fasting (such as Lent) or to celebrate after a period of religious observance – hence the Easter breads and cakes made throughout Europe. Cakes were also a way of making use of preserved fruits, citrus rinds, nuts and seeds – precious cargo brought back to this country by travellers and traders. Sometimes sweet and savoury ingredients were mixed, as in the earliest mince pies. Precious spices from the East helped preserve meat, and gradually cooks evolved ways of making a particular flavour the central theme of a cake.

The basic ingredients of cakes are fat, flour, sugar and eggs, with the exception of sponge cakes, which are fatless – although even then there are one or two sponge cakes that contain a small proportion of fat. The texture varies according to the method of preparation and the proportion of fat to flour. The richest cakes include equal proportions of the basic ingredients, as in a Victoria Sandwich.

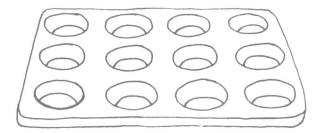

There are five standard methods of making cakes – Creaming, All-in-one, Rubbing-in, Melting and Whisking. Basic information about each of these methods is given at the beginning of the relevant chapters. Cakes are some of the trickiest things to cook and, inevitably, problems arise – especially when baking cakes for the first few times. You should persevere, however, and just learn by your mistakes because there is nothing more rewarding than being able to offer and eat a well-baked cake. The problems that may be encountered when baking cakes by the various methods are discussed in their chapters.

INGREDIENTS

ALCOHOL

The addition of a few tablespoons of alcohol – generally brandy, rum or sweet/dry sherry or Madeira – is popular. However, take care not to be too generous since too much liquid could result in an over-wet cake mixture which would not rise properly. When a cake is completely cold, you can pierce holes in it with a skewer and 'feed' it alcohol – usually this involves adding brandy or rum to a fruit cake. It enhances the flavour and gives the cake your own interpretation. Be careful, however, not to be over-enthusiastic or the cake will become soggy.

BAKING POWDER and BICARBONATE OF SODA, see RAISING AGENTS

BLACK TREACLE, GOLDEN SYRUP and HONEY

Because it is so difficult to weigh these correctly, measurements in this book are given in tablespoons rather than by weight

BUTTER, see FATS and OILS

CHOCOLATE

Chocolate for baking may be found on the home baking shelves of most supermarkets rather than on the confectionery shelves. There is usually a selection of milk, white and plain (bitter) chocolate, and chocolate chips.

Chocolate is any product that is obtained from fermented cocoa beans. The food laws in the UK cover the definition of chocolate and plain (bitter) must contain a minimum of 30% cocoa solids; obviously the more cocoa solids, the stronger the flavour. Continental dark chocolate will contain over 70% cocoa solids and will produce a most intense flavour in cakes and bis-cuits. Adding condensed or powdered milk or cream and sugar to the cocoa solids results in a more palatable milk chocolate.

Cocoa powder is a bitter-flavoured powder used in baking.

COCONUT

Coconut, the sweet white flesh obtained from the fruit of the coconut palm, is an excellent source of vitamins, protein and natural oils. As a baking ingredient, it is available flaked, shredded and desiccated.

COFFEE CONCENTRATE

This is bought in the coffee section in supermarkets, e.g. Camp coffee. However, you can make your own: for each 1 tablespoon required in the recipe, dissolve 1 teaspoon coffee powder in 1 tablespoon boiling water and allow to cool before using.

DRIED FRUIT, BASIC – CURRANTS, RAISINS, SULTANAS and GLACÉ CHERRIES

Easily available in packets from the supermarket, these may now be bought ready cleaned, but it is probably worthwhile sorting through the fruit to remove any stalks etc. Glacé cherries should be washed and dried.

DRIED FRUIT, EXOTIC – APRICOTS, DATES, MANGO, PAPAYA, PINEAPPLE and PRUNES

There are now new fruits available, such as mango and papaya, which add considerable excitement to cake making. These newer fruits have become more available as the countries from where they are imported have increased their production, and the drying processes have been modernised. The fruit in these packets is ready-to-eat and does not need soaking. If you buy the ordinary 'dried' fruit instead of the 'ready-to-eat' version, however, you will need to soak it in a little water for an hour to make it fleshy before adding to the cake mixture.

EGGS

These should be used at room temperature, and for all recipes in this book medium eggs have been used unless stated other-wise in the individual recipe.

FATS and OILS – BUTTER, LARD, MARGARINE, SPREADS

The information in this section is included to help you choose the best products for baking. First of all, it is important that the difference between a fat and an oil is understood.

The term 'fat' is used to describe a product that remains solid at room temperature. The most familiar fats are those derived from animals, such as lard, suet and dripping, and cream, which is churned into butter. Fats are used both in cooking and for spreading. In Britain, until the early 1900s, the fats used were largely derived from animals, specifically beef and pork fat.

Oils are the refined end product of a nut- or seed-crushing process, and are chiefly used for cooking – specifically for roasting, deep frying and stir frying – and for salad dressings, as they remain liquid at room temperature. The use of oils for cooking and dressings is popular in Mediterranean countries where, for centuries, the olive has yielded oil in various grades for all culinary purposes. During the second half of the twentieth century, new methods of extracting, refining and hardening oils from other sources has allowed spreads to be made of oils from fish, vegetables, nuts, herbs and plants – such as almond, coconut, corn or maize, cottonseed, palm, peanut, rapeseed, safflower, sesame seed, soya bean, sunflower and walnut.

BUTTER

Butter is a solid fat made by churning cream, first by separating it from the milk, and then pasteurising it to destroy enzymes and bacteria. Churning involves rapidly stirring the cream until the fat forms a solid mass which can be collected, washed and shaped. Butter must by law contain at least 78% fat and 20% whey or other milk products. Butter is available as salted, slightly salted or unsalted; it is labelled salted when it contains more than 1.5% salt. For all the recipes in this book I have used salted butter. As butter is perishable, it must be stored in the refrigerator.

Softened butter should be used when cakes and biscuits are made by the creaming and all-in-one methods. It can be left at room temperature for a short time before using. Do not allow it to become too soft, however, otherwise the cooked product will have an oily finish.

Chilled butter produces the best results when making cakes and biscuits by the melting or rubbing-in methods; use butter straight from the refrigerator.

LARD

Lard is extracted commercially from pigs' internal fat. Pure lard is 99% fat and will make cakes heavy if used alone; it is therefore best used with a mixture of butter or margarine.

MARGARINE

Margarine made from vegetable oils was first formulated ninety years ago and came onto the British market seventy years ago. During the Second World War, margarine was the universal alternative to butter on the daily bread, but has in recent years been superseded by spreads (see below). A full-fat margarine, which contains not less than 80% fat, will act in the same way as butter when spread or cooked with.

Hard margarines are made with a blend of hydrogenated fish oils and vegetable oils. The blend is perfect for baking, particularly for traditional methods – that is, when cakes are made by the creaming and the rubbing-in methods. Before creaming, hard margarine may be allowed to soften for a short time at room temperature; however, if it is allowed to become too soft, it becomes very oily during the mixing. Hard margarines produce more reliable results in rich fruit cakes than soft margarines, since they give more support to the cake structure, resulting in an even distribution of fruit.

Soft margarines are also made with a blend of hydrogenated fish oils and vegetable oils but are especially blended (emulsified) to give a softer consistency. It is most important that they should be used straight from the refrigerator, and not brought out into the warmth first. If soft margarines are allowed to soften before use, the cooked result will be poor. You can use soft margarines for all types of cakes but they are particularly good when making cakes by the all-in-one method.

SPREADS

Spreads have a lower fat content than margarines – somewhere between 60% and 80%. They are made from a mixture of ingredients: animal fats, hydrogenated fish oils, vegetable oils and dairy ingredients, according to the individual brand.

Packet spreads are best used straight from the refrigerator and perform well in traditional cake and pastry making. Like hard margarines, they are an alternative to butter.

Tub spreads are best used straight from the refrigerator. They are excellent when used for making cakes by the all-in-one method but are not recommended for rich fruit cakes since the cakes do not keep as well as those made with a full-fat margarine.

ALTERNATIVES TO ANIMAL PRODUCTS

For those who wish to avoid animal fats or other ingredients of animal origin, either for religious, dietary or cultural reasons, there are margarines and spreads available which are made from the vegetable, nut and herb oils mentioned above. Similarly, for those unable to tolerate milk products, there are milk-free varieties available.

The labels on the packaging will give you information on the types and levels of fats contained in the product, together with the individual ingredients. Use this information to help you to choose the correct proportions of fat in your diet.

FLOUR

It is always a good idea to sieve flour before using it; this will ensure that any impurities are sieved out, and that it mixes better with the other ingredients.

White self-raising flour has raising agents thoroughly mixed into the flour so that a consistent end result is obtained. It is suitable for most cakes and most biscuits. This flour should not be used when cakes are made by the whisking method.

White plain flour is suitable for most cakes when used with the addition of a raising agent (see below). It is the best choice for rich fruit cakes. It can, however, be used for cakes without the addition of a raising agent in recipes where air is incorporated by whisking.

Wholemeal flour may be substituted for white flour. For a lighter cake, use half wholemeal and half white flour.

Sponge flour is finely milled from an especially 'soft' wheat, to give a higher rise and finer texture to sponges and light cakes.

Cornflour is a very soft white flour derived from maize; it is used in cakes and biscuits to give a light, short texture.

Polenta is an Italian golden cornmeal produced from maize.

FRESH FRUIT – APPLES, BANANAS, CITRUS, PEARS, PLUMS

Always choose good-looking fruit although since most will be peeled, the odd blemish on the skin will not matter. However, when the zest of citrus fruit – lemons, limes and oranges – is to be used, try to buy fruit with unwaxed skins.

FRUIT, DRIED, see DRIED FRUIT, BASIC and EXOTIC

JAM

When jam is required – to sandwich between two cakes, perhaps, or as part of the main cake itself – there is no need to sieve it. However, if using jam to brush over a cake before placing marzipan or icing on the top, best results will be achieved by sieving the jam first.

LARD, see FATS and OILS

MARGARINE, see FATS and OILS

MIXED PEEL, CANDIED

Fruit peel is preserved by placing it into a strong sugar solution; it is then removed and dried. The sugar remaining on the peel acts as a preservative.

OATMEAL

After the removal of the bran, the oat grain is ground into coarse, medium or fine oatmeal. For all the recipes in this book, I have used medium.

NUTS – ALMONDS, BRAZILS, PECANS, WALNUTS

These are all available, shelled, in packets from supermarkets. Almonds, already skinned, are available whole, flaked or ground. Brazils and pecans are available whole. Walnuts are available as halves or in pieces and the latter are especially useful when they are to be chopped.

RAISING AGENTS

Air incorporated during the mixing is, of course, the primary raising agent but, unless a flour which includes a raising agent is used, air alone is rarely enough and an additional aid is required. There are three commercial varieties available:

Bicarbonate of soda is an alkaline substance which gives off carbon dioxide to assist with the rising of food.

Cream of tartar is an acidic substance which is usually mixed two parts to one part bicarbonate of soda, and reacts to release the carbon dioxide slowly. giving a more even rise. It leaves behind a tasteless salt in the food.

Baking powder is a mixture of the two, blended with dried starch to prevent the reaction of the two mixtures whilst the baking powder is stored.

SPREADS, see FATS and OILS

SUGAR

It is well known that sugar is a good source of energy and is speedily digested. Commercially prepared sugars are all available as refined white or unrefined golden.

Caster sugar is a fine-grain sugar and is the variety mostly used for baking.

Granulated sugar does not dissolve as easily as caster sugar, and in baking is most used for sprinkling over cakes as a topping.

Icing sugar is a finely-ground powder and mostly used for making icings.

Demerara sugar is a moist golden crystal sugar and is most often used for sprinkling over cakes and biscuits before baking.

Soft light and dark brown sugar refers to any fine moist brown sugar made from refined sugar combined with molasses. It is commonly used in baking. Using light or dark brown sugar gives a different flavour, texture and colour to cakes than caster sugar would.

Muscovado (or Barbados) sugar is unrefined 'raw' cane sugar, available as light or dark. It is usually finely grained and gives cakes and biscuits a deeper flavour.

Molasses sugar is raw sugar that contains most goodness and the highest amount of natural molasses. It is very dark and sticky. It has an exceptionally strong molasses flavour and is ideal for rich fruit cakes.

CAKE TINS

To avoid disasters, it is important that you use the correct cake tin for the recipe you wish to cook, and when selecting cake tins, the depth (the height of the sides of the tin) and diameter (the distance across the top of the tin) are both important. All the cake tins in the recipes that follow will be at least 7.5 cm (3 inches) in depth unless otherwise stated. The measurement in the recipes refers to the diameter: for example,' a 20 cm (8-inch) round cake tin' will measure 20 cm (8 inch) across and be 7.5 cm (3 inches) high. If you use a cake tin with a small diameter than the recipe states, the mixture will be denser and take longer to cook; conversely, if you use a cake tin with a larger diameter than the recipe states, the mixture will be shallower and will cook more quickly.

THE TINS USED IN THIS BOOK ARE:

Round: see above.

Square: as above, with a usual depth of 7.5 cm (3 inches) Both of the above tins are available with fixed bases, with removable bases or in a spring clip version: all are suitable for making cakes. However, always ensure that the base of a spring clip tin is firmly and securely in position before lining the tin and adding the cake mixture.

Sandwich: a round tin, with a usual depth of 4 cm (1½ inches).

Loaf: a rectangular tin, sold in 450 g (1 lb) or 900 g (2 lb) sizes.

Swiss roll: a rectangular tin, with a usual depth of 2 cm (¾ inch).

Tube: is usually 23 cm (9 inches) in diameter with a tube through the centre of it, making a ring shape; it is usually 4 cm (1½ inches) deep.

LINING TINS

For most cake tins (unless they are non-stick), it is necessary to line them with either greaseproof or silicone-coated paper. For rich mixtures and fruit cakes, completely line the tins. However when cooking the Victoria Sandwich Cake, Apple and Raisin Cake, or Energy Bars, it is usually sufficient to line the base of the tin only.

To line a round tin: Cut a piece of greaseproof paper long enough to fit around the inside of the tin and overlap slightly; this strip should be at least 5 cm (2 inches) deeper than the tin. Fold over one of the long sides of this strip by about 2.5 cm (1 inch), creasing it firmly; then snip this piece at 2.5 cm (1-inch) intervals, which will ensure the paper fits neatly. Brush the inside of the strip lightly with cooking oil and place it into the tin with the cut edge flat against the base. Stand the tin on a piece of greaseproof paper and draw a circle round it; then cut out the circle with scissors. Brush the base of the tin lightly with oil and fit the base paper into the bottom of the tin, over the top of the cut edge of the side paper.

To line a sandwich tin: Stand the tin on a piece of greaseproof paper and draw round it and then cut out the shape with scissors. Brush the base of tin lightly with oil and fit the paper into the bottom of the tin. Brush the sides of the tin with oil.

To line a loaf tin: Cut an oblong of greaseproof paper the length of the base and sides of the loaf tin. Grease the tin and line it by placing the paper over the top of the tin, then pressing down in the middle and pushing out into the corners.

To line a Swiss roll tin: Cut a piece of greaseproof paper that is about 2.5 cm (1 inch) bigger on each side than the tin. Place the tin in the centre of this piece of paper and in each corner make a cut at an angle so that, when fitted into the tin, the paper fits neatly and closely overlaps at the corners. Lightly grease the tin and fit the paper.

TEMPERATURES & TIMINGS

Fan ovens do not need preheating unless a recipe specifically tells you to do this. Cooking times are quicker in a fan oven than a conventional oven. Although few cookery books give a different setting for fan ovens, expecting cooks to consult their cooker handbooks, temperatures are given for fan ovens in all recipes in this book.

Inevitably, each oven varies in its efficiency so to obtain the best results from your oven, it may be necessary to adjust the instructions for cooking temperatures given in the recipes in this book: gas settings may have to be varied by one Gas Mark and electric or fan ovens by 10–20°C. See also the Guide to Perfect Baking opposite, which gives tips on how to tell when the cake is ready.

When following the cooking times given in the recipes, use the approximate middle time if you are cooking in a gas or electric oven: i.e. if the time given is 10–20 minutes, check the cake at 15 minutes. When cooking in a fan oven, always check the cake at the earliest time: if the time given is 10–20 minutes, check at 10 minutes.

ELECTRIC MIXERS

An electric mixer is a great help when making cakes: they are either hand-held or part of a larger machine. Always remember to start mixing on a low speed and increase the speed as the mixture blends together. Scrape down the blades and side of the bowl regularly to ensure the ingredients mix evenly. Fold in the flour and any other ingredients by hand to ensure that the air that has been incorporated during the mixing remains in the mixture.

A food processor may be used to make cakes and biscuits, but cakes will tend not to rise as well as if they had been made by hand or using an electric mixer. Remember when adding fruit only to blend lightly or the blade will chop the fruit too finely.

OVENS

Conventional electric ovens and gas ovens need to be preheated for 15 minutes before cakes are placed in them. It is important that the shelves in electric and gas ovens are correctly positioned since this can be critical to the success of the cake. Since the correct shelf positions vary with every oven, it is recommended that you consult your cooker handbook for guidance. It is equally important to remember to position the shelves correctly before preheating so that when the oven reaches the required temperature, the door is not left open for longer than necessary while shelves are adjusted.

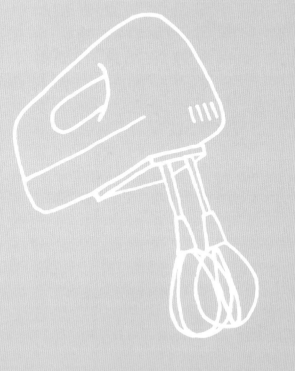

GUIDE TO PERFECT BAKING

CAKES

1 Take care to weigh all ingredients accurately to ensure the proportions are correct. Remember to use either metric or imperial measures, and never mix the measurements. This is one of the few areas of cooking where accuracy is essential.

2 A light cake relies on air being incorporated into the mixture during the first part of the preparation stage. When making a cake by the all-in-one method, baking powder as well as self-raising flour will need to be used. This is necessary since no air is incorporated during the mixing as in the case of traditional creaming.

3 Sometimes when making a creamed mixture, adding the eggs to the fat and sugar too quickly can cause the mixture to curdle. To help overcome this, add 1 tablespoon of the flour from the list of ingredients and continue to add the eggs slowly

4 When spooning the mixture into the cake tin before cooking, smooth the top with the back of a metal spoon; this will help ensure that the cooked cake rises evenly.

5 Always bake cakes as soon as the ingredients are mixed. This is especially important with those cakes that use baking powder as the raising agent since this starts to work as soon as it comes into contact with moisture.

6 Always space the oven shelves evenly so air can circulate properly. When cooking more than one cake in an conventional electric or gas oven (but not a fan oven), it will be necessary to remove the top one first and place the lower one on top to complete its cooking. This will usually be for an additional 5–20 minutes, depending on the type of cake; cook until it is golden in colour and firm to the touch.

7 To prevent cakes sinking, never open the oven door during the early part of the cooking; in fact, try to avoid opening the oven door until at least half the cooking time has elapsed.

8 To test if a cake is cooked, press the centre lightly with the fingertip. A cooked cake should be springy and give only very slightly to the pressure, then rise immediately leaving no impression. I was always encouraged to listen to a fruit cake to hear if it had stopped singing; however, I find the best and truly only way of being able to tell if a deep (with a depth of approximately 7.5 cm/3 inches) cake is cooked through is to use a thin cake skewer. Push the skewer into the centre of the cake and if it is cooked, the skewer should come out clean. If there is any cake mixture on the skewer, the cake will require additional cooking; I would give a cake an extra few minutes before trying again.

9 When a cake is cooked, each recipe will give advice on how long to leave the cake in the tin before taking it out; this will allow the cake to shrink slightly away from the sides so it will be more easily removed. It will also be firmer and therefore easier to handle.

10 To remove the cake from the tin, gently run a knife around the edge of the cake tin. Turn out the cake onto a wire rack, remove any paper and place right side up on a wire cooling rack. When a cake has a light, fragile top, turn it out onto a wire cooling rack covered with a clean tea towel, cover with another cooling rack and invert both racks together and remove the top rack. This also avoids marking the top, which is important if entering cakes in a show for judging.

11 All cakes must be quite cold before storing otherwise mould will develop. Cakes keep best in clean, airtight tins. A sponge should be eaten within two days, a Victoria Sandwich will keep for up to a week, but a rich fruit cake will keep for months in a tin made completely airtight – its keeping qualities can be improved even further by brushing the top with alcohol. Alternatively, cakes may be wrapped in double greaseproof paper, then in a sheet of foil, and a polythene bag or an airtight polythene box and stored in a cool dry place. Instructions for storage are not given for each recipe unless specific to that recipe.

12 Most cakes freeze satisfactorily but it is important to follow a few rules. Having baked the cake and allowed it to cool completely (see above), completely wrap it in either clingfilm or a polythene bag. Wrap cake layers separately, using greaseproof or silicone paper between the layers. Do not fill the cake with jam, buttercream or cream before it is frozen. Thaw a small cake for 1–2 hours, larger cakes for 3–4 hours. There is no need to freeze rich fruit cakes since these keep well if properly wrapped.

BISCUITS & COOKIES

Biscuits are traditionally crisp and dry, and there are six main definitions of biscuit: bar, drop, piped, refrigerator, rolled and shaped. Cookies have a softer texture and are usually sweeter than biscuits; they originated in North America.

1 If the recipe requires the ingredients to be melted together, use a gentle heat so that the mixture does not overheat.

2 For the best results when cooking biscuits and cookies, use flat baking trays without high sides since high sides prevent proper browning.

3 Always leave space on the baking trays between the biscuits and cookies to enable them to spread. Cookies do not need to be even in shape.

4 Always space the oven shelves evenly so air can circulate properly. When cooking more than one tray in an conventional electric or gas oven (but not a fan oven), it will be necessary to remove the top tray first and place the lower one on top to complete its cooking. This will usually be for an additional 5–10 minutes, depending on the type of biscuit; cook until they are golden in colour.

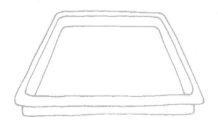

5 When baked, the biscuits and cookies should be left to cool on the baking tray to allow them to set; this helps stop them breaking. Then remove them with a flat, wide spatula to wire racks to cool completely.

6 Store biscuits and cookies in an airtight container lined with non-stick paper and place a sheet of non-stick paper between each layer.

7 If biscuits have a filling, sandwich them together just before serving. To add the filling before storing will turn the biscuits soggy.

MEASUREMENTS

OVEN TEMPERATURES

Gas Mark	Electric (°C)	Fan oven (°C)
	80	60
	90	70
	100	80
E	110	90
1	120	100
1	130	110
1	140	120
2	150	130
3	160	140
3	170	150
4	180	160
5	190	170
6	200	180
6	210	190
7	220	200
8	230	210
9	240	220
9	250	230

NOTE: These temperatures are equivalent settings rather than exact conversions of degrees of heat.

VOLUME MEASURES

$1/4$ teaspoon	1.25 ml
$1/2$ teaspoon	2.5 ml
1 teaspoon	5 ml
2 teaspoons	10 ml
1 tablespoon	15 ml

NOTE: When teaspoons/tablespoons are used for measuring dry ingredients, these should be rounded (as much of the ingredient above as in the bowl of the spoon). Measuring spoons should be filled only so the top surface is level.

VOLUME MEASURES

Imperial (fluid ounces/pints)	Metric (millilitres/litres)
1 fl oz	25 ml
2 fl oz	50 ml
3 fl oz	80 ml
4 fl oz	115 ml
5 fl oz/$1/4$ pint	150 ml
6 fl oz	175 ml
7 fl oz	200 ml
8 fl oz	225 ml
9 fl oz	250 ml
10 fl oz/$1/2$ pint	300 ml
11 fl oz	325 ml
12 fl oz	350 ml
13 fl oz	375 ml
14 fl oz	400 ml
15 fl oz/$3/4$ pint	425 ml
16 fl oz	450 ml
17 fl oz	475 ml
18 fl oz	500 ml
19 fl oz	550 ml
20 fl oz/1 pint	575 ml
$1 1/4$ pints	700 ml
$1 1/2$ pints	850 ml
$1 3/4$ pints	1 litre
2 pints	1.1 litres
$2 1/4$ pints	1.3 litres
$2 1/2$ pints	1.4 litres
$2 3/4$ pints	1.6 litres
3 pints	1.7 litres
$3 1/4$ pints	2 litres

NOTE: The measurements are equivalents, not exact conversions. Always follow either the imperial or the metric measures and do not mix the two in one recipe.

WEIGHT MEASURES

Imperial (ounces/pounds)	Metric (grams/kilograms)
1 oz	25 g
2 oz	50 g
3 oz	80 g
4 oz	115 g
5 oz	150 g
6 oz	175 g
7 oz	200 g
8 oz	225 g
9 oz	250 g
10 oz	275 g
11 oz	300 g
12 oz	350 g
13 oz	375 g
14 oz	400 g
15 oz	425 g
16 oz	450 g
1 lb 1 oz	475 g
1 lb 2 oz	500 g
1 lb 3 oz	525 g
1 lb 4 oz	550 g
1 lb 5 oz	600 g
1 lb 6 oz	625 g
1 lb 7 oz	650 g
1 lb 8 oz	675 g
2 lb	900 g
3 lb	1.3 kg
3 lb 5 oz	1.5 kg

This is the most traditional method of cake making.

The fat and sugar are beaten together until the mixture is light in colour and fluffy in texture and the sugar has been incorporated. A large number of air cells are produced which are stabilised by the sugar. More air cells are introduced by beating eggs into the fat and sugar mixture. The flour should be folded in gently so that no air is lost; it is unlikely that sieving in the flour will incorporate additional air.

THE CREAMING METHOD

During baking, the fat melts and the raising agent in the flour reacts with the liquid from the egg to produce carbon dioxide and steam. As pressure builds up inside the cake, these gases transfer to the air cells formed during mixing and allow the cake to rise. By the end of the baking time, this movement has ceased, as the proteins in the flour and eggs are set. The cooked cake consists of a large number of air cells surrounded by a network of proteins in which starch granules are held. The texture of a cake made by the creaming method is a little closer and finer than an all-in-one cake.

 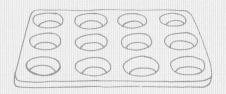 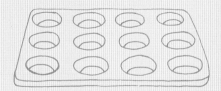

PROBLEMS THAT CAN OCCUR WITH CAKES MADE BY THE CREAMING METHOD, AND REMEDIES

HOLLOW TOP
- Too much raising agent: check proportions.
- Over-creaming in mixer or food processor: mix for less time since this will reduce risk of removing air from the mixture.
- Too cool an oven: adjust temperature.
- Insufficient cooking: adjust cooking time.

DOMED TOP
- Mixture insufficiently creamed together before eggs added: cream mixture for longer to incorporate fat and sugar together.
- Cake baked too high in oven: adjust shelf position.
- Oven temperature too high: adjust temperature.

COARSE TEXTURE
- Too much raising agent: check proportions.
- Flour unevenly mixed into mixture before cooking: fold in flour slowly and thoroughly.

CLOSE, DAMP TEXTURE
- Mixture too slack before cooking, caused by too much liquid, too little flour or too much sugar: check proportions.
- Mixture insufficiently creamed together before eggs added: cream mixture for longer to incorporate fat and sugar together.
- Oven temperature too low: adjust temperature.

COLLAR EDGE ON BAKED CAKE
- Too much raising agent: check proportions.
- Fan oven preheated: place in cold fan oven.
- Cake has risen too rapidly and sunk, caused by cake being baked too high in oven: adjust shelf position.

SUGAR SPOTTING
- Wrong type of sugar used: check recipe and sugar type used.
- Insufficient creaming so sugar remains undissolved: cream mixture for longer before adding eggs.

RISEN UNEVENLY
- Mixture unevenly spread in tin: ensure mixture is spread evenly.
- Tin warped during cooking: buy a heavier gauge of tin.
- Oven shelves not level: adjust using a spirit level.

CAKE SUNK IN CENTRE
- Too much raising agent: check proportions.
- Fan oven preheated and too hot: place cake in cold fan oven and check temperatures.

MAKES 8–10 slices
PREPARATION TIME: 20 minutes +
covering 25–30 minutes
COOKING TIME: 40–50 minutes

This famous sponge cake, traditionally made with pink and yellow squares and covered with marzipan, is sometimes called Window Cake or Tennis Cake, the last name because the squares resemble the layout of a tennis court. For a change, here is a version made with chocolate squares.

FOR THE CAKE
175 g (6 oz) butter, softened
175 g (6 oz) caster sugar
3 eggs
225 g (8 oz) self-raising flour, sieved
1 teaspoon vanilla essence
115 g (4 oz) milk chocolate, melted
2 tablespoons warmed raspberry jam, sieved

FOR THE COVERING
115 g (4 oz) ground almonds
115 g (4 oz) icing sugar, sieved
1 egg, beaten lightly
1 teaspoon lemon juice
$^{1}/_{2}$ teaspoon almond essence

1 Cream together the butter and the sugar until light and fluffy.
2 Beat in the eggs. Fold in the flour.
3 Divide the mixture into two bowls. Into one, stir the vanilla essence; into the other, stir the melted chocolate. Mix thoroughly.
4 Grease and line an 18 cm (7-inch) square cake tin. Divide the tin in half with folded greaseproof paper.
5 Place each of the mixtures in one half of the prepared tin; smooth the tops.
6 Bake at Gas Mark 4/electric oven 180°C/fan oven 160°C for 40–50 minutes until golden in colour and springy to the touch.
7 Remove the cake from the tin, carefully remove the paper from between the two halves and separate into the two halves. Place them on a wire rack to cool completely.
8 Divide each cake in half, down the length.
9 To cover the cake, first spread each of the length's sides evenly with the warm jam, which should hold the four pieces together, and assemble into a square with alternate colours on each side.
10 Make the covering by mixing the covering ingredients together; knead gently.
11 Roll out the covering on a surface lightly dusted with icing sugar.
12 Cut a strip long enough to fit the top, bottom and two sides. Then cut 2 squares to fit the remaining 2 sides. Remember to smooth the edges to give a neat finish.
Dust with icing sugar.

BATTENBERG CAKE

MAKES 12–16 slices
PREPARATION TIME: 20 minutes
COOKING TIME: 45–60 minutes

CARDAMOM & LEMON CAKE

Cardamom is a member of the ginger family. It has small husks that contain tiny seeds, which have a strong bitter-sweet and slightly lemony flavour. The seeds can be crushed or ground in a spice or coffee grinder or in a pestle and mortar.

225 g (8 oz) butter, softened
225 g (8 oz) caster sugar
4 eggs
sieve together: 350 g (12 oz) plain flour
    and 2 teaspoons baking powder
10 cardamom pods, seeds removed and ground coarsely
grated zest and juice of 2 unwaxed lemons
50 g (2 oz) ground almonds

1   Cream the butter and sugar until light and fluffy.
2   Beat in the eggs; fold in the flour and baking powder.
3   Stir in the cardamom, zest and the juice of the lemons and the ground almonds.
4   Spoon the mixture into a greased and lined 20 cm (8-inch) round cake tin; smooth the top.
5   Bake at Gas Mark 4/electric oven 180°C/fan oven 160°C for 45–60 minutes until golden in colour and springy to the touch.
6   Leave the cake in the tin for 10 minutes; then remove from the tin and leave it on a wire rack until completely cool.

MAKES 20–24 slices
PREPARATION TIME: 2–4 hours marinating + 30 minutes
COOKING TIME: 2–2¹/₂ hours

CHAIRMAN'S CAKE

This cake was designed for Mrs Eileen Meadmore in celebration of her term of office as NFWI National Chairman. It has become one of my all-time favourite cakes.

115 g (4 oz) glacé cherries, halved
175 g (6 oz) ready-to-eat dried apricots, chopped
115 g (4 oz) ready-to-eat dried pineapple, chopped
115 g (4 oz) raisins
115 ml (4 fl oz) Drambuie
100 g (3¹/₂ oz) brazil nuts, chopped roughly
100 g (3¹/₂ oz) walnut pieces, chopped roughly
150 g (5 oz) butter, softened
150 g (5 oz) dark muscovado sugar
225 g (8 oz) set honey
4 eggs
175 g (6 oz) plain flour, sieved
115 g (4 oz) ground almonds
200 g (7 oz) dark plain chocolate, cut into chunks

1   Place the prepared cherries, apricots, pineapple and raisins in a bowl, add the Drambuie, cover and leave to stand for 2–4 hours.
2   At the end of the marinating time, add the nuts to the fruit mixture.
3   Cream the butter and sugar together in a large bowl until light and fluffy. Stir in the honey; then beat in each egg separately.
4   Fold in the flour and ground almonds, mixing well.
5   Carefully stir in the fruit, nuts and chocolate.
6   Spoon the mixture into a greased and lined 23 cm (9-inch) round cake tin.
7   Bake at Gas Mark 2/electric oven 150°C/fan oven 130°F for 2–2¹/₂ hours or until a skewer inserted in the centre comes out clean. Remove from the oven and leave in the tin until cool.
8   This cake is best stored for 5–7 days, well wrapped in foil, before being eaten.

MAKES 12–16 slices
PREPARATION TIME: 15–20 minutes
COOKING TIME: 1¼–1½ hours

CHERRY CAKE

This is one of my favourite cakes. It is a delight when cut since the cherries give colour to this almond-flavoured cake.

225 g (8 oz) butter, softened
225 g (8 oz) caster sugar
4 eggs
sieve together: 225 g (8 oz) plain flour
    and ½ teaspoon baking powder
250 g (9 oz) glacé cherries, quartered
115 g (4 oz) ground almonds
a few drops almond essence
1 tablespoon milk
2 tablespoons demerara sugar

1 Cream the butter and sugar together until light and fluffy.
2 Lightly whisk the egg and beat it in a little at a time. Using a metal spoon, carefully fold the flour and baking powder into the creamed mixture.
3 Gently fold the cherries and ground almonds into the cake, adding one or two drops of almond essence and then the milk.
4 Spoon the cake mixture into a greased and lined 20 cm (8-inch) round cake tin, level off the top with the back of a spoon, then sprinkle with the demerara sugar.
5 Bake at Gas Mark 4/electric oven 180°C/fan oven 160°C for 1¼–1½ hours or until the centre of the cake is springy to the touch.
6 Cool the cake in the tin for 15 minutes before turning it out on to a wire rack to cool completely.

MAKES 16–20 slices
PREPARATION TIME: 30–40 minutes
COOKING TIME: 1¾–2 hours

TROPICAL FRUIT CAKE

The mix of tropical fruits, marzipan and orange produces a handsome, modern cake.

175 g (6 oz) butter, softened
175 g (6 oz) caster sugar
3 eggs
50 g (2 oz) ready-to-eat dried mango, chopped
50 g (2 oz) ready-to-eat dried papaya, chopped
50 g (2 oz) glacé cherries, halved
50 g (2 oz) glacé pineapple, chopped
225 g (8 oz) sultanas
115 g (4 oz) walnut pieces, roughly chopped
115 g (4 oz) marzipan, cut into 12 pieces
grated zest and juice of 2 unwaxed oranges
sieve together: 115 g (4 oz) plain flour
    and 115 g (4 oz) plain wholemeal flour
    and 1 teaspoon baking powder
    and 2 teaspoons ground cinnamon
25 g (1oz) flaked almonds (optional)

1 Cream the butter and sugar together until light in colour and fluffy. Gradually beat in the eggs.
2 Stir in the prepared fruits, walnuts and marzipan.
3 Fold in the zest and juice of the oranges, the flours, baking powder and cinnamon.
4 Spoon the mixture into a greased and lined 20 cm (8-inch) round cake tin, level the top and sprinkle over the flaked almonds if required.
5 Bake at Gas Mark 2/electric oven 150°C/fan oven 130°F for 1½–2 hours until the cake is firm, dark golden and a skewer inserted in the centre of the cake comes out clean.
6 Leave the cake to cool in the tin for 15 minutes before turning it out onto a wire rack to cool completely.

CHOCOLATE, WALNUT & BANANA LOAF *opposite*

MAKES 10–12 slices
PREPARATION TIME: 20 minutes
COOKING TIME: 1–1½ hours

115 g (4 oz) butter
175 g (6 oz) caster sugar
2 large bananas, peeled and mashed
2 eggs
sieve together: 80 g (3 oz) plain flour
and 80 g (3 oz) plain wholemeal flour
and 1 teaspoon bicarbonate of soda
and 1 teaspoon ground cinnamon
5 tablespoons boiling water
115 g (4 oz) walnut pieces, chopped
175 g (6 oz) milk chocolate chips

The chocolate, banana and walnuts used in this cake give it respectively a tasty, moist and crunchy texture.

1 In a large bowl, beat the butter and sugar together until light and creamy. Beat in the bananas and then the eggs; don't worry if the mixture looks curdled.
2 Fold in the flours, bicarbonate of soda and cinnamon. Stir in the boiling water, this will produce a soft mixture.
3 Gently fold in the walnuts and the chocolate chips.
4 Spoon the mixture into a greased and lined 900 g (2 lb) loaf tin and smooth the top.
5 Bake at Gas Mark 4/electric oven 180°C/fan oven 160°C for 1–1½ hours until dark golden in colour and well risen.
6 Leave the cake in the tin for 10 minutes before placing it on a wire rack to cool completely.

WALNUT-TOPPED SULTANA & APRICOT CAKE

MAKES 12–16 slices
PREPARATION TIME: 50 minutes including soaking fruit
COOKING TIME: 1¼–1½ hours

175 g (6 oz) sultanas
115 g (4 oz) ready-to-eat dried apricots, chopped
4 tablespoons Grand Marnier
225 g (8 oz) butter, softened
225 g (8 oz) molasses sugar
4 eggs
sieve together: 225 g (8 oz) self-raising flour
and 2 teaspoons ground mixed spice
50 g (2 oz) walnut pieces, chopped

The fruit soaked in **alcohol** provides a moist base for this delicious cake.

1 Place the sultanas and apricots in a bowl, add the Grand Marnier and leave to soak for 30 minutes.
2 Cream the butter and sugar together until paler in colour and fluffy.
3 Beat in the eggs, fold in the flour and the spice, and then stir in the soaked fruit plus any remaining liquid.
4 Place the mixture in a greased and lined 20 cm (8-inch) round cake tin; smooth the top. Sprinkle the chopped walnuts evenly over the top.
5 Bake at Gas Mark 4/electric oven 180°C/fan oven 160°C for 1¼–1½ hours until golden and firm to the touch.
6 Remove the cake from the oven and leave it in the tin for 10 minutes before placing it on a wire rack to cool completely.

MAKES approximately 30
PREPARATION TIME: 15–20 minutes
COOKING TIME: 20–25 minutes

These cookies have the texture
of shortbread.

sieve together: 250 g (9 oz) plain flour
   and 115 g (4 oz) icing sugar
225 g (8 oz) butter, softened
1 egg yolk
1 teaspoon almond essence
100 g (3½ oz) blanched almonds, chopped
100 g (3½ oz) chocolate chips

ALMOND &
CHOCOLATE COOKIES

1   Place the flour and icing sugar in a bowl,
   beat in the butter and egg yolk until light
   and creamy.
2   Mix in the almond essence, chopped
   almonds and chocolate chips thoroughly.
3   Take walnut-sized pieces of the dough
   and roll into balls, place on greased
   baking trays and flatten slightly.
4   Bake at Gas Mark 3/electric oven
   160°C/fan oven 140°C for 20–25
   minutes until the cookies are pale in
   colour and firm.
5   Leave the cookies to stand on the trays
   for 5 minutes before placing them on
   wire racks to cool.

MAKES 10–12 slices
PREPARATION TIME: 25–30 minutes
COOKING TIME: 50–70 minutes

For a good flavour use Bramley apples.
Prepare apples last to avoid browning.

175 g (6 oz) butter, softened
175 g (6 oz) molasses sugar
2 eggs
sieve together:
   150 g (5 oz) wholemeal self-raising flour
   and 115 g (4 oz) self-raising flour
350 g (12 oz) cooking apples, peeled,
   cored and diced
80 g (3 oz) pecan nuts, roughly chopped
juice of 1 orange

APPLE, ORANGE &
PECAN CAKE

1   Cream the butter and the sugar together
   until light in colour and fluffy.
2   Beat in each egg, then fold in the flours,
   stir in the prepared apples and the
   pecans, together with the orange juice.
3   Spoon the mixture into a greased and
   lined 900 g (2 lb) loaf tin; smooth its top.
4   Bake at Gas Mark 4/electric oven
   180°C/fan oven 160°C for 50–70
   minutes, until the cake is well risen and
   firm to the touch.
5   Allow the cake to cool in the tin for 15
   minutes before placing it on a wire rack
   to cool completely.

MAKES 12–16 slices
PREPARATION TIME:
30 minutes soaking + 15 minutes.
COOKING TIME: 2½–3 hours

The sultanas are soaked in the alcohol and
retain the flavour after cooking – a delicious
moist cake.

450 g (1 lb) sultanas
200 ml (7 fl oz) Marsala sweet wine
225 g (8 oz) butter, softened
350 g (12 oz) caster sugar
4 eggs
sieve together: 350 g (12 oz) plain flour
   and 2 teaspoons baking powder
1 teaspoon almond essence

BOOZY SULTANA
CAKE

1   Soak the sultanas in the Marsala for at
   least 30 minutes.
2   Cream the butter and the sugar together
   until light in colour and fluffy. Beat in the
   eggs separately.
3   Fold in the flour and the baking powder,
   mixing well.
4   Stir in the soaked sultanas with any
   remaining liquid, and the almond essence.
5   Spoon the mixture into a greased and
   lined 20 cm (8-inch) round cake tin;
   smooth the top.
6   Bake at Gas Mark 2/electric oven
   150°C/fan oven 130°F for 2½–3 hours
   until dark golden-brown. A skewer
   pushed into the centre of the cake
   should come out clean.
7   Leave the cake to stand in the tin for 15
   minutes before placing it on a wire rack
   to cool completely.

MAKES 18
PREPARATION TIME: 20 minutes
COOKING TIME: 15–20 minutes

These biscuits have a light, melting texture with masses of chocolate flavour.

125 g (4¹/₂ oz) unsalted butter, softened
80 g (3 oz) icing sugar
sieve together: 175 g (6 oz) self-raising flour
    and 25 g (1 oz) cornflour
    and 2 tablespoons cocoa powder
80 g (3 oz) milk chocolate,
    melted and cooled

TO FINISH
115 g (4 oz) milk chocolate, melted

CHOCOLATE VIENNESE

1 Cream the butter and sugar together until light in colour and fluffy
2 Gradually beat in the flours and cocoa powder, then beat in the melted and cooled chocolate. Knead the mixture to form a soft dough.
3 Take small quantities of the dough and roll them into walnut-size balls; place them on greased baking trays and flatten slightly.
4 Bake at Gas Mark 4/electric oven 180°C/fan oven 160°C for 15–20 minutes until they are firm to the touch. Place them on a wire rack to cool completely.
5 To finish, dip the base of each biscuit into the melted chocolate and place on parchment paper to dry.

MAKES 12–16 slices
PREPARATION TIME: 15 minutes
COOKING TIME: 50–60 minutes

This Madeira-type cake contains poppy seeds, which give it a nutty flavour, while the addition of lime and lemon juice gives it a fresh taste. Poppy seeds are available from supermarkets or health food shops.

250 g (9 oz) butter, softened
200 g (7 oz) caster sugar
grated zest and juice of 2 unwaxed limes
grated zest and juice of 1 unwaxed lemon
4 eggs
300 g (11 oz) self-raising flour, sieved
2 tablespoons poppy seeds

CITRUS POPPY SEED CAKE

1 Cream the butter and sugar in a large bowl until light in colour and fluffy. Beat in the zest of the limes and the lemon.
2 Beat in the eggs, then fold in the flour followed by the lime and lemon juice and the poppy seeds.
3 Spoon into a greased and lined 20 cm (8-inch) round cake tin, and smooth the top.
4 Bake at Gas Mark 3/electric oven 160°C/fan oven 140° for 50–60 minutes.
5 When cooked, leave the cake in the tin for 15–20 minutes before placing it on a wire rack to cool completely.

MAKES 12–16 slices
PREPARATION TIME: 45 minutes
COOKING TIME: 1–1¹/₄ hours

The soaking of the fruit gives this light-textured cake a delicious orange flavour.

115 ml (4 fl oz) Cointreau
115 ml (4 fl oz) freshly squeezed orange juice
225 g (8 oz) ready-to-eat dried apricots, finely chopped
115 g (4 oz) sultanas
175 g (6 oz) butter, softened
3 tablespoons clover honey
4 eggs, separated
sieve together: 175 g (6 oz) self-raising flour
    and 2 teaspoons baking powder

APRICOT & ORANGE CAKE

1 Place the orange liqueur, orange juice, apricots and sultanas in a saucepan and bring to the boil. Remove from the heat and leave to cool.
2 Cream together the butter and the honey until well blended.
3 Beat in the egg yolks. Fold in the flour and baking powder, and then gradually mix in the fruit.
4 In a clean, grease-free bowl whisk the egg whites until stiff; fold into the cake mixture.
5 Spoon the mixture into a greased and lined 20 cm (8-inch) round cake tin; smooth the top.
6 Bake at Gas Mark 4/electric oven 180°C/fan oven 160°C for 1–1¹/₄ hours until it is pale golden in colour and springy to the touch.
7 Leave to cool completely in the tin.

MAKES 8–12 slices
PREPARATION TIME:
25 minutes +10 minutes icing
COOKING TIME: 25–35 minutes

The potato in this cake gives it a **moist texture**; I think you will find that everyone will be amazed that this contains potato. You can get the chocolate-coated coffee beans in most good confectioners or delicatessens.

80 g (3 oz) butter, softened
200 g (7 oz) caster sugar
115 g (4 oz) mashed potato, warm
30 ml (2 tablespoons) double cream
1 tablespoon cocoa powder
3 eggs, separated
sieve together: 80 g (3 oz) self-raising flour
and 1 teaspoon baking powder
2 tablespoons milk, if required

FOR THE ICING
225 g (8 oz) icing sugar, sieved
2 tablespoons cocoa powder, sieved
50 g (2 oz) butter, softened
2 tablespoons coffee concentrate
2 tablespoons rum
chocolate-coated coffee beans

1 Cream the butter and sugar together until well blended.
2 Mash the potato with the double cream and cocoa powder; then stir this into the creamed mixture. Beat in the egg yolks, and stir in the flour and baking powder. If the mixture is rather stiff, add enough milk to give a dropping consistency.
3 In a clean grease-free bowl, whisk the egg whites until stiff; then gently fold them into the mixture.
4 Divide the mixture between two greased and lined 18 cm (7-inch) sandwich tins and smooth the top.
5 Bake at Gas Mark 5/electric oven 190°C/fan oven 170°C for 25–35 minutes until springy and set.
6 Cool the cakes in the tins for 10 minutes before turning them out onto a wire rack to cool completely.
7 To make the icing, place the icing sugar and cocoa in a bowl, beat in the butter, then stir in the coffee and rum.
8 Use the icing to sandwich the two halves of the cake together, and then spread the remainder over the top and sides. Decorate the top with chocolate-covered coffee beans.

CHOCOLATE POTATO CAKE

MADEIRA CAKE

PREPARATION TIME: 10–20 minutes
COOKING TIME: see table below

This rich cake would have been served with a glass of Madeira in Victorian times.
It is often referred to as a plain cake because it contains no fruit and is only flavoured with
lemon, but there is nothing to beat a really good Madeira cake. It can be served plain or cut in
half and filled with a jam of your choice, then covered with marzipan and iced for a celebration
(page 43).

The table indicates the quantities of ingredients required to make Madeira cakes to fit the
standard range of square and round tins. If you want to make a shaped cake, such as a number
or heart, you need to know how much mixture is required to fill the special tin. This is quite
simple to calculate: simply fill the tin with water to the depth you require the cake to be,
measure the water, and then look on the chart.

1 Cream the butter and sugar together until light in colour and fluffy.
2 Sift the flours together.
3 Beat the eggs, one at a time, into the creamed mixture.
4 Fold in the flour with the grated lemon zest and juice.
5 Spoon the mixture into the prepared greased and lined tin; smooth the top.
6 Bake at Gas Mark 3/electric oven 160°C/fan oven 140°C for the length of time given on the chart until well risen, firm to touch and golden in colour
7 Allow the cake to cool in the tin for 5–10 minutes, then turn out on a wire rack to cool completely.

For a tin of this size:								
square tin (side)	13 cm (5 inches)	15 cm (6 inches)	18 cm (7 inches)	20 cm (8 inches)	23 cm (9 inches)	25 cm (10 inches)	28 cm (11 inches)	30 cm (12 inches)
round tin (diameter)	15 cm (6 inches)	18 cm (7 inches)	20 cm (8 inches)	23 cm (9 inches)	25 cm (10 inches)	28 cm (11 inches)	30 cm (12 inches)	33 cm (13 inches)
approx liquid capacity of cake tin	300 ml (¹/₂ pint)	700 ml (1¹/₄ pints)	1 litre (1³/₄ pints)	1.1 litres (2 pints)	1.7 litres (3 pints)	2 litres (3¹/₂ pints)	2.5 litres (4¹/₂ pints)	3 litres (5¹/₄ pints)
You will need these quantities:								
butter, softened	50 g (2 oz)	115 g (4 oz)	175 g (6 oz)	225 g (8 oz)	275 g (10 oz)	350 g (12 oz)	400 g (14 oz)	450 g (16 oz)
caster sugar	50 g (2 oz)	115 g (4 oz)	175 g (6 oz)	225 g (8 oz)	275 g (10 oz)	350 g (12 oz)	400 g (14 oz)	450 g (16 oz)
self-raising flour	50 g (2 oz)	115 g (4 oz)	175 g (6 oz)	225 g (8 oz)	275 g (10 oz)	350 g (12 oz)	400 g (14 oz)	450 g (16 oz)
plain flour	25 g (1 oz)	50 g (2 oz)	80 g (3 oz)	115 g (4 oz)	150 g (5 oz)	175 g (6 oz)	200 g (7 oz)	225 g (8 oz)
eggs	1	2	3	4	5	6	7	8
grated zest and juice of unwaxed lemon	¹/₄	¹/₂	1	1	1¹/₂	1¹/₂	2	2
approx. cooking time in minutes	35–45	60–75	75–90	75–90	75–90	75–90	75–90	80–100

WEDDING CAKE WITH A DIFFERENCE

18 cm (7-inch) cake will give 30 slices
23 cm (9-inch) cake will give 60 slices
PREPARATION TIME:
soaking the fruit overnight + 40–60 minutes
COOKING TIME: 2¼–3½ hours

Two friends, Jane and Mark, were getting married and they asked me to develop a cake that was modern in style and reflected their love of travelling. **Boiling and then soaking in alcohol the wonderful selection of exotic and traditional dried fruits makes this cake most unusual.** The result is a moist, flavour-filled fruit cake.

	18 cm (7-inch) square	23 cm (9-inch) square
raisins	450 g (1 lb)	675 g (1 lb 8 oz)
sultanas	225 g (8 oz)	350 g (12 oz)
currants	225 g (8 oz)	350 g (12 oz)
crystallised pineapple, diced	115 g (4 oz)	175 g (6 oz)
crystallised papaya, diced	115 g (4 oz)	175 g (6 oz)
glacé cherries, chopped	115 g (4 oz)	175 g (6 oz)
rum	150 ml (5 fl oz)	175 ml (6 fl oz)
red wine	250 ml (9 fl oz)	400 ml (14 fl oz)
butter, softened	225 g (8 oz)	350 g (12 oz)
soft dark brown sugar	225 g (8 oz)	350 g (12 oz)
eggs	5	8
black treacle	1 tablespoon	2 tablespoons
sieve together:		
plain flour	225 g (8 oz)	350 g (12 oz)
and ground cinnamon	1 teaspoon	1½ teaspoons
and ground mixed spice	1 teaspoon	1½ teaspoons
desiccated coconut	80 g (3 oz)	125 g (4½ oz)

1 In a large saucepan, place the raisins, sultanas, currants, pineapple, papaya, and glace cherries. Add the rum and red wine, bring to the boil, reduce the heat and simmer for 15 minutes. Stir constantly until the liquid has evaporated.

2 Cover and leave to stand for at least 6 hours or overnight to allow the fruit to absorb the moisture.

3 Cream together the butter and the sugar until light in colour and fluffy. Beat in the eggs and the black treacle.

4 Fold in the flour, spices and coconut; mix well.

5 Stir in the marinated fruit, mixing thoroughly.

6 Spoon the mixture into the required size of greased and lined tin. Smooth the top.

7 Bake at Gas Mark 3/electric oven 160°C/fan oven 140°C for 2½–3½ hours, depending on the size of the cake, until it is dark golden and a skewer inserted in the centre comes out clean.

8 Leave the cake in the tin for at least 1 hour to cool and set before placing it on wire rack to cool completely.

9 Wrap the cake in greaseproof paper and foil. Store for at least 4 weeks before covering with marzipan and decorating with icing as desired (page 43).

GOLDEN FRUIT CAKE *pictured opposite*

MAKES 12–16 slices
PREPARATION TIME:
1–2 hours soaking fruit + 30 minutes
COOKING TIME: 1¼–1½ hours

350 g (12 oz) mixed ready-to-eat
dried exotic fruit
250 ml (9 fl oz) fruit tea
(made using two teabags)
175 g (6 oz) butter, softened
175 g (6 oz) caster sugar
3 eggs
225 g (8 oz) self-raising flour, sieved
2 tablespoons milk
25 g (1oz) shredded coconut

FOR THE TOPPING
80 g (3 oz) icing sugar, sieved
5 teaspoons boiling water
15 g (½ oz) shredded coconut

This cake uses the ready-to-eat exotic dried fruits which are now available, such as mango, papaya, pear and pineapple. Try using differently flavoured fruit teas to give variety to the flavour.

1 Soak the fruit in the tea for 1–2 hours. Drain.
2 Cream the butter and sugar until light in colour and fluffy. Gradually beat in each egg, then fold in the flour and milk.
3 Fold in the fruit and coconut; mix well.
4 Spoon the mixture into a greased and lined 20 cm (8-inch) round cake tin; smooth the top.
5 Bake at Gas Mark 4/electric oven 180°C/fan oven 160°C for 1¼–1½ hours until it is well risen and golden, and a skewer inserted into the centre comes out clean.
6 Let the cake cool in the tin for 10 minutes, then turn it onto a wire rack to cool completely.
7 To make the topping, place the icing sugar into a bowl and gradually beat in the boiling water to give a smooth, thick icing. Spread the icing over the top of the cake. Scatter over shredded coconut.

SHORTBREAD

MAKES approximately 20 slices
PREPARATION TIME: 20 minutes
COOKING TIME: 40–50 minutes

225 g (8 oz) butter, softened
115 g (4 oz) icing sugar
sieve together: 225 g (8 oz) plain flour
***and* 115 g (4 oz) cornflour**
caster sugar, to dredge

This is a truly melt-in-the-mouth recipe.

1 Cream together the butter and sugar until creamy and paler in colour.
2 Blend in the flour and cornflour until thoroughly mixed.
3 Place the mixture into a well-greased 33 x 23 cm (13- x 9-inch) Swiss roll tin. Using floured hands, press down so the mixture is evenly spread in the tin. Prick with a fork.
4 Bake at Gas Mark 2/electric oven 150°C/fan oven 130°F for 40–50 minutes until pale golden in colour.
5 Remove the shortbread from the oven, dredge generously with caster sugar, and then cut into fingers.
6 Leave the shortbread to stand for 10 minutes before placing the fingers on a wire rack to cool completely.
7 Stored in an airtight container, they will stay crisp for up to 2 weeks.

MAKES 10–12 slices
PREPARATION TIME: 15 minutes
COOKING TIME: 60–75 minutes

This is a moist cake that always reminds me of eating fresh dates in summer and walnuts at Christmas.

80 g (3 oz) ready-to-eat dates,
    roughly chopped
80 g (3 oz) walnut pieces, roughly chopped
175 g (6 oz) margarine, softened
175 g (6 oz) soft dark brown sugar
3 eggs
225 g (8 oz) self-raising flour, sieved
2 tablespoons granulated sugar (optional)

MAKES 10–12 slices
PREPARATION TIME: 20 minutes
COOKING TIME: 1–1¼ hours

Try different flavoured honeys: I particularly like Caribbean clover honey.

175 g (6 oz) butter, softened
80 g (3 oz) caster sugar
80 g (3 oz) set honey
2 eggs
sieve together: 115 g (4 oz) plain flour
    and 115 g (4 oz) wholemeal flour
    and 2 teaspoons baking powder
50 g (2 oz) ground almonds
115 g (4 oz) glacé cherries, quartered
2–3 tablespoons milk

MAKES 10–12 slices
PREPARATION TIME: 10–15 minutes
COOKING TIME: 50–65 minutes

The lemon juice and sugar poured over the cooked cake produces a crunchy glaze and gives it a tangy flavour.

175 g (6 oz) butter, softened
175 g (6 oz) caster sugar
2 eggs
4 tablespoons milk
175 g (6 oz) self-raising flour, sieved
grated zest and juice of 1 unwaxed lemon
1 tablespoon icing sugar

DATE & WALNUT CAKE

1. In a bowl, cream the margarine and sugar together until pale in colour and fluffy.
2. Add the eggs one at a time, beating well. Fold in the flour and the prepared dates and walnuts.
3. Spoon the mixture into a greased and lined 900 g (2 lb) loaf tin; smooth the top. The top may be sprinkled with granulated sugar.
4. Bake at Gas Mark 4/electric oven 180°C/fan oven 160°C for 60–75 minutes until firm to the touch and dark golden in colour.
5. Leave to cool in the tin for 10 minutes before turning onto a rack to cool completely.

HONEY & CHERRY CAKE

1. Cream the butter, sugar and the honey together until light in colour and fluffy; however, be careful not to over beat.
2. Beat in the eggs. Then fold in the flours, baking powder, ground almonds and the cherries.
3. Stir in enough milk to give a soft mixture.
4. Spoon the mixture into a greased and lined 900 g (2 lb) loaf tin.
5. Bake at Gas Mark 3/electric oven 160°C/fan oven 140°C for 60–75 minutes until the cake is well risen, firm to the touch, and dark golden in colour.
6. Leave the cake in the tin for 10 minutes before placing it on a wire rack to cool completely.

LEMON DRIZZLE CAKE

1. Cream the butter and sugar together until light in colour and fluffy. Gradually beat in the eggs and milk.
2. Fold the flour into the mixture with the grated lemon zest.
3. Spoon the mixture into a greased and lined 900 g (2 lb) loaf tin.
4. Bake at Gas Mark 4/electric oven 180°C/fan oven 160°C for 50–65 minutes until the cake is golden-brown and firm to the touch.
5. Mix the lemon juice and icing sugar together and pour over the cake as soon as it is removed from the oven. Allow the glaze to set before removing the cake from the tin. Set on a wire rack to cool completely.

MAKES approximately 16
PREPARATION TIME: 10 minutes
COOKING TIME: 10–15 minutes

These are lightly textured cookies which melt in the mouth. To produce half an egg, beat a whole egg and then use half – or make double the quantity of these delicious cookies.

80 g (3 oz) margarine, softened
25 g (1 oz) lard
80 g (3 oz) caster sugar
¹/₂ egg, beaten
¹/₂ teaspoon vanilla essence
150 g (5 oz) self-raising flour, sieved
50 g (2 oz) rolled oats
a few glacé cherries, chopped

MAKES 16–20 slices
PREPARATION TIME: 15–20 minutes
COOKING TIME: 2³/₄–3¹/₄ hours

Evaporated milk produces a moist fruit cake with a rich, creamy taste.

225 g (8 oz) butter, softened
225 g (8 oz) soft light brown sugar
3 eggs
sieve together: 275 g (10 oz) plain flour
   and 1 teaspoon baking powder
250 g (9 oz) currants
250 g (9 oz) sultanas
250 g (9 oz) raisins
115 g (4 oz) glacé cherries, halved
115 ml (4 fl oz) evaporated milk

MAKES 12–16 slices
PREPARATION TIME: 25 minutes
COOKING TIME: 60–75 minutes

A mixture of coffee and chocolate flavours makes this a very popular cake.

225 g (8 oz) butter, softened
225 g (8 oz) caster sugar
4 eggs
225 g (8 oz) self-raising flour, sieved

TO FINISH
2 tablespoons coffee concentrate
115 g (4 oz) milk chocolate, melted

MELTING MOMENTS

1 Cream the margarine, lard and sugar together until light in colour and fluffy. Beat in the egg and vanilla essence.
2 Stir in the flour, mixing well together.
3 Shape the mixture into walnut-sized balls, then roll the balls in oats to coat them thoroughly.
4 Place the balls on lightly greased baking trays. Flatten them slightly with the palm of the hand and place a small piece of chopped glacé cherry on each biscuit.
5 Bake at Gas Mark 4/electric oven 180°C/fan oven 160°C for 10–15 minutes.
6 Leave them to cool on baking trays for 5 minutes before placing them on wire racks to cool completely.

MILKY FRUIT CAKE

1 Cream the butter and sugar together until light in colour and fluffy.
2 Beat in each egg; fold in the flour and baking powder.
3 Stir in the dried fruit, glacé cherries and evaporated milk; mix thoroughly.
4 Place the mixture in a greased and lined 20 cm (8-inch) round cake tin; smooth the top.
5 Bake at Gas Mark 3/electric oven 160°C/fan oven 140°C for 2³/₄–3¹/₄ hours until golden in colour and set and a skewer inserted into the centre comes out clean.
6 Leave to stand in the tin for 30 minutes before placing the cake on a wire rack to cool completely.

MOCHA MARBLE CAKE

1 Cream the butter and sugar together until light in colour and fluffy.
2 Beat in the eggs, then fold in the flour, being sure to obtain an even mixture.
3 Divide the mixture between two bowls. Add the coffee to one bowl and the melted chocolate to the other bowl.
4 In a greased and lined 20 cm (8-inch) round cake tin, place alternate spoonfuls of the mixtures around the tin, then repeat, placing alternate spoonfuls on top. Using the spoon, swirl the mixture together gently in order to mix it slightly.
5 Bake at Gas Mark 3/electric oven 160°C/ fan oven 140°C for 60–75 minutes until the cake has risen well, is dark golden-brown and firm to the touch.
6 Leave the cake to stand in the tin for 10 minutes before turning it out onto a wire rack to cool completely.

FRUIT COOKIES *pictured opposite*

MAKES 24
PREPARATION TIME: 15–20 minutes
COOKING TIME: 20–25 minutes

80 g (3 oz) butter, softened
80 g (3 oz) soft light brown sugar
1 egg
175 g (6 oz) self-raising flour, sieved
1 teaspoon almond essence
8 cardamom pods, seeds removed
from husks and crushed
50 g (2 oz) glacé cherries, finely chopped
50 g (2 oz) ready-to-eat dried apricots,
finely chopped
50 g (2 oz) glacé ginger, finely chopped

The bitter-sweet flavour of the cardamom (page 18) and the hot sweetish flavour of the ginger produce a delicious lightly flavoured fruit cookie.

1 Cream the butter and sugar until light in colour and fluffy. Beat in the egg.
2 Stir in the remaining ingredients to form a stiff dough.
3 Using two teaspoons, make small rounds. Place on lightly greased baking sheets, and flatten slightly.
4 Bake at Gas Mark 4/electric oven 180°C/fan oven 160°C for 20–25 minutes until pale golden in colour.
5 When cooked, place on a wire rack to cool completely.

VICTORIA SANDWICH

SERVES 8–12 slices
PREPARATION TIME: 15 minutes
COOKING TIME: 20–30 minutes

175 g (6 oz) hard margarine
175 g (6 oz) caster sugar
3 eggs
175 g (6 oz) self-raising flour, sieved

FOR THE FILLING
90 ml (6 tbsp) raspberry jam

This English cake became popular during Queen Victoria's reign. The original version was baked in an oblong Yorkshire pudding tin and then sandwiched together with jam and cut into fingers.

1 Cream the margarine and sugar together until light in colour and fluffy. Beat in the eggs.
2 Gently fold the flour into the mixture.
3 Grease and base line two 18 cm (7-inch) sandwich tins. Divide the mixture equally between the tins. Smooth the tops.
4 Bake at Gas Mark 4/electric oven 180°C/fan oven 160°C for 20–30 minutes until they are golden brown and springy to the touch.
5 Leave the cakes to stand in the tins for 5 minutes before placing them on a wire rack to cool completely.
6 When cold, sandwich the two halves together with raspberry jam. Dust the top of the cake with caster sugar.

CHOCOLATE VICTORIA SPONGE: Mix together 2 tablespoons cocoa powder and 3 tablespoons boiling water to make a paste and allow to cool. Then stir it gently into the mixture.

LEMON VICTORIA SPONGE: Stir in the grated zest and juice of an unwaxed lemon.

MAKES: 18–20
PREPARATION TIME: 15 minutes soaking + 15 minutes
COOKING TIME: 15 minutes

SPICY BRANDY COOKIES

The moist raisins give these spicy cookies a soft texture.

50 g (2 oz) raisins, chopped
2 tablespoons brandy
175 g (6 oz) butter, softened
115 g (4 oz) granulated sugar
50 g (2 oz) soft dark brown sugar
4 tablespoons milk
sieve together: 225 g (8 oz) plain flour
and **¹/₂ teaspoon bicarbonate of soda**
and **1 teaspoon ground cinnamon**
and **1 teaspoon finely ground nutmeg**
finely grated zest of 1 unwaxed orange

1 Soak the raisins in the brandy for 15 minutes, until almost all the liquid has been absorbed.
2 Cream the butter and sugars together until light in colour and fluffy. Stir in the milk, raisins, then the flour, bicarbonate of soda and the spices. Add the grated orange zest. Mix everything together well.
3 Using a teaspoon, place small mounds of the mixture on greased baking trays, leaving room for them to spread.
4 Bake at Gas Mark 4/electric oven 180°C/fan oven 160°C for 10–15 minutes until the cookies are pale golden.
5 Allow the cookies to stand on trays for 5 minutes before placing them on wire racks to cool completely.
6 Stored in an airtight container, these will keep for up to one week.

MAKES 12–16 slices
PREPARATION TIME: 20 minutes
COOKING TIME: 1–1¹/₄ hours

APRICOT, PINEAPPLE & NUT CAKE

Using the flavoured ale gives this fruit cake a new twist. The ale can usually be found on the alcohol shelves in the supermarket.

225 g (8 oz) butter, softened
350 g (12 oz) soft dark brown sugar
3 tablespoons set honey
2 eggs
450 g (1 lb) plain flour, sieved
115 g (4 oz) ready-to-eat dried apricots, diced
115 g (4 oz) crystallised pineapple, diced
175 g (6 oz) chopped mixed nuts
2 teaspoons bicarbonate of soda
2 teaspoons ground cinnamon
about 250 ml (9 fl oz) cherry-flavoured ale

1 Cream together the butter, sugar and the honey until light and fluffy. Beat in the eggs.
2 Fold in the flour, then the fruit, nuts, bicarbonate of soda and the cinnamon.
3 Add enough ale to produce a soft dropping mixture.
4 Spoon the mixture into a greased and lined 23 cm (9-inch) round cake tin; smooth the top.
5 Bake at Gas Mark 4/electric oven 180°C/fan oven 160°C for 1–1¹/₄ hours until a skewer inserted into the centre of the cake comes out clean.
6 Leave the cake in the tin until it is completely cold.

MAKES approximately 20
PREPARATION TIME: 20 minutes + 1 hour in refrigerator
COOKING TIME: 15–20 minutes

BARBARA'S COOKIES

This is a favourite recipe of Barbara Gill, a member of the NFWI's Board of Trustees, and uses an original mixture of potato, almonds, cherries and a blend of spices.

115 g (4 oz) butter, softened
115 g (4 oz) soft light brown sugar
1 tablespoon golden syrup
80 g (3 oz) potato, peeled and finely grated
25 g (1 oz) flaked almonds, chopped
25 g (1 oz) glacé cherries, chopped
sieve together: 175 g (6 oz) self-raising flour
    and 50 g (2 oz) wholemeal self-raising flour
    and ¹/₂ teaspoon ground nutmeg
    and ¹/₂ teaspoon ground mixed spice
    and ¹/₂ teaspoon ground cinnamon

1 In a bowl cream together the butter and sugar until light and fluffy.
2 Stir in the syrup, potato, almonds and cherries; mix well.
3 Fold in the flour and spices. Place the mixture, covered, in the refrigerator for at least 1 hour.
4 Remove from the refrigerator and place the mixture on a well-floured surface. Roll it into a sausage shape approximately 4 cm (1¹/₂ inches) in diameter.
5 Using a sharp knife, cut the mixture into 15 mm (¹/₂-inch) slices. Place these on greased baking trays.
6 Bake at Gas Mark 6/electric oven 200°C/fan oven 180°C for 15–20 minutes.
7 Leave to stand on the trays for 5 minutes before placing the cookies on wire racks to cool.

MAKES approximately 16
PREPARATION TIME: 10–15 minutes
COOKING TIME: 10–20 minutes

BASIC DROP COOKIES

This recipe has a soft dropping mixture, which is easy to make and bake.

80 g (3 oz) margarine, softened
80 g (3 oz) caster sugar
1 egg
sieve together: 225 g (8 oz) plain flour
    and ¹/₂ teaspoon baking powder
3 tablespoons milk
¹/₂ teaspoon vanilla essence

1 Cream the margarine and sugar together until fluffy, then beat in the egg.
2 Stir in the flour, baking powder, milk and vanilla essence to form a soft dough. The mixture should not be too soft, so add the milk carefully since it may not all be needed.
3 Drop teaspoonfuls of the mixture onto greased baking trays, leaving enough room for the cookies to spread.
4 Bake at Gas Mark 4/electric oven 180°C/fan oven 160°C for 10–20 minutes.
5 Leave to stand on the trays for 5 minutes before placing the cookies on wire racks to cool completely.

VARIATIONS: Substitute soft light brown sugar for the caster sugar to make light brown cookies.
Add 80 g (3 oz) mixed dried fruit and 25 g (1 oz) chopped nuts.
Add 1 teaspoon ground cinnamon to the dry mixture.
Substitute 1 tablespoon cocoa powder for the same amount of the flour.

MAKES 12–16 slices
PREPARATION TIME: 40–45 minutes +
60 minutes for fruit to stand
+ 15 minutes to complete
COOKING TIME: 2–2½ hours

This spiced fruit cake has a layer of marzipan in the centre, and another on the top. **Originally, the cake was baked by girls in service to take home with them on Mothering Sunday**. It is now more usual to have Simnel cake at Easter time, with eleven almond-paste eggs on the top, representing the Apostles but omitting Judas.

This is a modern variation and is extremely tasty.

FOR THE MARZIPAN
225 g (8 oz) ground almonds
225 g (8 oz) caster sugar
115 g (4 oz) icing sugar, sieved
1 egg, separated
juice of ½ lemon

FOR THE CAKE
175 g (6 oz) raisins
175 g (6 oz) sultanas
80 g (3 oz) glacé cherries, chopped
80 g (3 oz) walnut pieces, chopped
115 ml (4 fl oz) stout
175 g (6 oz) butter, softened
175 g (6 oz) soft dark brown sugar
3 eggs
sieve together: 225 g (8 oz) plain flour
***and* ½ teaspoon baking powder**
***and* 1 teaspoon ground mixed spice**

TO FINISH
3 tablespoons apricot jam, sieved

1 First make the marzipan. Mix the ground almonds and sugars. Add the egg yolk, lemon juice and enough egg white to mix to a stiffish paste. Retain the rest of the egg white.
2 Wrap the marzipan in clingfilm and put in the refrigerator.
3 Place the raisins, sultanas, glacé cherries, walnut pieces and stout in a saucepan and heat until steaming. Remove from the heat; allow to stand for 60 minutes.
4 Cream the butter and sugar until light in colour and fluffy; then gradually beat in the eggs.
5 Fold in the flour, baking powder and spice. Carefully stir in the soaked fruit with its liquid.
6 Grease and line an 18 cm (7-inch) round cake tin, place half the mixture in the tin and smooth the top.
7 Roll out one-third of the marzipan into a 18 cm (7-inch) circle, and place it on the top of the mixture in the tin. Add the remaining cake mixture and smooth the top.
8 Cook at Gas Mark 3/electric oven 160°C/fan oven 140°C for 2–2½ hours until pale golden, and a skewer inserted into the centre of the cake comes out clean.
9 Leave the cake to stand in the tin for 15 minutes before turning it out onto a wire tray to cool completely.
10 When cold, remove the lining paper and brush the top of the cake with apricot jam.
11 Roll out half the remaining marzipan to fit top of the cake and press in position.
12 Score the surface of the marzipan to make a diamond pattern and brush with the remaining egg white.
13 Roll the remaining marzipan into eleven even-sized balls and press around the rim of the top of the cake; brush with egg white.
14 Place the cake under a preheated grill and toast gently until the marzipan is golden brown.

SIMNEL CAKE

MAKES approximately 36
PREPARATION TIME: 15 minutes
COOKING TIME: 15–20 minutes

CHOCOLATE BANANA COOKIES

These cookies have a crisp texture and a flavoursome blend of ingredients. Banana chips are available in the home-baking section at the supermarket.

250 g (9 oz) butter, softened
150 g (5 oz) soft dark brown sugar
100 g (3¹/₂ oz) granulated sugar
2 eggs
1 teaspoon vanilla essence
1 large banana, peeled and mashed
sieve together: 350 g (12 oz) plain flour
    and 1 teaspoon bicarbonate of soda
115 g (4 oz) chocolate chips
80 g (3 oz) banana chips, coarsely chopped

1   Cream the butter and sugars together until light in colour and fluffy.
2   Beat in the eggs and essence. Stir in the mashed banana. Fold in the flour and bicarbonate of soda, mixing thoroughly.
3   Stir in the chocolate and banana chips.
4   Drop large teaspoonfuls of the mixture onto greased baking sheets, making sure you leave space for the mixture to spread out.
5   Bake at Gas Mark 5/electric oven 190°C/fan oven 170°C for 15–20 minutes until golden-brown.
6   Remove the cookies from the oven, leaving them on the baking sheets for a few minutes before placing them on a wire rack to cool completely.
7   Store in airtight container; they should keep for two weeks.

MAKES 10–12 slices
PREPARATION TIME: 20–25 minutes
COOKING TIME: 1¹/₄–1¹/₂ hours

CHOCOLATE CRUNCHY CAKE

Chunks of dark chocolate are placed on the top of the cake, melting into the cake during the cooking. The cake is delicious when served warm with ice cream as a dessert.

175 g (6 oz) butter, softened
175 g (6 oz) caster sugar
2 eggs, beaten
5 tablespoons cocoa powder, sieved
175 ml (6 fl oz) milk
sieve together: 225 g (8 oz) plain flour
    and 1¹/₂ teaspoons bicarbonate of soda
115 g (4 oz) plain chocolate, broken into chunks

1   Cream together the butter and sugar until light and fluffy. Beat in the eggs.
2   In a separate bowl, mix the cocoa and half the milk into a smooth paste, and then stir in the remaining milk to form a runny liquid.
3   Stir in half the amalgamated flour and bicarbonate of soda and then half the cocoa mixture; repeat. Mix well together to produce a very slack mixture.
4   Pour the mixture into a greased and lined 20 cm (8-inch) round cake tin. Place the chunks of chocolate on top of the cake.
5   Bake at Gas Mark 4/electric oven 180°C/fan oven 160°C for 1¹/₄–1¹/₂ hours.
6   The cake will be well risen and springy to the touch when cooked. Leave it in the tin for at least 30 minutes before turning it out and placing on a wire rack to cool.

MAKES 12
PREPARATION TIME: 10–15 minutes
COOKING TIME: 15–25 minutes

CHOCOLATE KISSES

These cocoa-flavoured cookies are quick and easy to make, and will prove a hit with adults and children.

115 g (4 oz) butter, softened
80 g (3 oz) caster sugar
1 egg yolk
2 tablespoons milk
2 tablespoons cocoa powder, dissolved in 2 tablespoons boiling water
sieve together: 225 g (8 oz) plain flour
   and 1 teaspoon baking powder

FOR THE BUTTERCREAM FILLING
80 g (3 oz) butter, softened
sieve together: 175 g (6 oz) icing sugar
   and 1 tablespoon cocoa powder

1 In a large bowl, beat the butter and sugar together until light and fluffy. Beat in the egg yolk, milk and cooled cocoa liquid.
2 Fold in the flour and baking powder to form a stiff mixture.
3 Place 24 small heaps of the mixture on greased baking sheets, remembering to give them room to spread.
4 Bake at Gas Mark 4/electric oven 180°C/fan oven 160°C for 15–25 minutes until set and dark golden. Transfer the cookies to a wire rack to cool.
5 To make the buttercream filling, beat together the butter, icing sugar and cocoa until light and fluffy. Sandwich two chocolate kisses together with the filling, and continue with the rest.
6 Chocolate kisses will last about 3–4 days before the filling turns them soggy.

MAKES 12–16 slices
PREPARATION TIME: 30 minutes
COOKING TIME: 45–60 minutes

NUT & POLENTA CAKE

This is a light-textured cake flavoured with nuts and honey. Try different flavoured honeys for a change.

80 g (3 oz) walnut pieces
80 g (3 oz) brazil nuts
150 g (5 oz) butter, softened
150 g (5 oz) soft dark brown sugar
4 tablespoons set honey
2 eggs
sieve together: 50 g (2 oz) plain flour
   and 50 g (2 oz) wholemeal flour
   and 1 teaspoon baking powder
   and 1 teaspoon ground nutmeg
1 teaspoon vanilla essence
5 tablespoons milk
65 g (2½ oz) polenta

1 Place the walnut pieces and brazil nuts on a baking tray. Roast at Gas Mark 6/electric oven 200°C/fan oven 180°C for 10 minutes. Allow to cool, then roughly chop.
2 Cream the butter, sugar and honey until light in colour and fluffy. Gradually beat in the eggs.
3 Fold in the flours, baking powder, nutmeg and vanilla essence.
4 Stir in the milk, polenta and the chopped nuts.
5 Place the mixture in a greased and lined 20 cm (8-inch) round cake tin.
6 Bake at Gas Mark 4/electric oven 180°C/fan oven 160°C for 45–60 minutes, until golden brown, well risen and set.
7 Leave to cool in the tin for 15 minutes, before placing the cake onto a wire rack to cool completely.

WHISKY SPICE CAKE *pictured opposite*

MAKES 12–16 slices
PREPARATION TIME:
1 hour including the soaking of the fruit
COOKING TIME: 50–70 minutes

225 g (8 oz) raisins
5 tablespoons whisky
5 tablespoons water
115 g (4 oz) butter, softened
115 g (4 oz) soft light brown sugar
2 eggs
sieve together: 225 g (8 oz) plain flour
and **1 teaspoon bicarbonate of soda**
and **1 teaspoon ground mixed spice**
115 g (4 oz) walnut pieces, roughly chopped

FOR THE BUTTERCREAM FILLING
115 g (4 oz) butter, softened
225 g (8 oz) icing sugar, sieved
2 tablespoons whisky
25 g (1oz) walnut pieces, roughly chopped

Soaking the raisins in the whisky syrup produces a moist, light-textured cake.

1   Place the raisins, whisky and water in a small saucepan and heat until steaming; then remove from the heat and leave to stand for 30 minutes.
2   Cream the butter and sugar together until light in colour and fluffy. Beat in the eggs.
3   Fold in the flour, bicarbonate of soda and the spice. Stir in the raisins and any remaining liquid; add the walnuts and mix thoroughly.
4   Place the mixture in a greased and lined 20 cm (8-inch) round cake tin; smooth the top.
5   Bake at Gas Mark 3/electric oven 160°C/fan oven 140°C for 50–70 minutes until golden and firm to the touch.
6   Remove the cake from the oven and leave it in the tin for 10 minutes before placing it on a wire rack to cool completely.
7   To make the buttercream, beat together the butter and the icing sugar until creamy. Stir in the whisky and the walnuts.
8   Cut the cake in half through the middle and then sandwich the two halves together with the buttercream. Spread the remainder over the top and the sides.
9   Stored in an airtight container, the cake will keep for 2–3 days.

PECAN OAT BISCUITS

MAKES approximately 16
PREPARATION TIME: 10–15 minutes
COOKING TIME: 10–20 minutes

115 g (4 oz) butter, softened
80 g (3 oz) soft dark brown sugar
1 egg
50 g (2 oz) porridge oats
50 g (2 oz) pecan nuts, finely chopped
sieve together: 80 g (3 oz) plain flour
and **¹/₂ teaspoon baking powder**

These crunchy oat biscuits are ideal with a cup of coffee

1   Cream the butter and sugar together until light in colour and fluffy.
2   Beat in the egg and then stir in the oats, nuts, flour and baking powder. Mix well to a soft dough.
3   Drop large teaspoonfuls of the mixture onto greased baking sheets, being sure to give them room to spread a little.
4   Bake at Gas Mark 4/electric oven 180°C/fan oven 160°C for 10–20 minutes until they are pale golden in colour. Put them to cool on a wire rack.
5   Stored in an airtight container, they will remain crisp for about a week.

RICH FRUIT CAKE

MAKES 16–24 slices
PREPARATION TIME: overnight soaking of
fruit + 25–30 minutes
COOKING TIME: 2½–3 hours

675 g (1 lb 8 oz) mixed dried fruit
85 g (3 oz) glacé cherries, cut in half
5 tablespoons rum
grated zest and juice of 1 unwaxed orange
150 g (5 oz) butter, softened
150 g (5 oz) soft dark brown sugar
3 eggs
sieve together: 175 g (6 oz) self-raising flour
and **1 teaspoon ground mixed spice**
50 g (2 oz) ground almonds

A traditional blend of fruit soaked in rum and orange produces a moist cake which is **ideal as a Christmas cake** if covered with marzipan and royal or fondant icing (see below), or with a selection of exotic glacé fruits.

1   In a bowl, place the dried fruit, glacé cherries, rum and zest and juice of the orange, stir well, cover and leave overnight.

2   Cream together the butter and sugar until soft. Beat in the eggs, then stir in flour, ground mixed spice and ground almonds; combine well.

3   Gradually stir in the fruit mixture, ensuring it is thoroughly mixed.

4   Place in a greased and lined 20 cm (8-inch) round cake tin; smooth the top.

5   Bake at Gas Mark 1/electric oven 140°C/fan oven 120°C for 2½–3 hours until dark golden and firm to the touch and a skewer inserted into the centre comes out clean.

6   Leave the cake in the tin for at least 30 minutes before removing it to a wire rack to cool completely.

MARZIPAN

MAKES: 450 g (1 lb) marzipan
PREPARATION TIME: 25 minutes, including placing the marzipan on the cake

115 g (4 oz) icing sugar, sieved
115 g (4 oz) caster sugar
225 g (8 oz) ground almonds
1 egg
½ teaspoon almond essence
2–4 tablespoons lemon juice

TO APPLY MARZIPAN
6 tablespoons apricot jam,
  sieved and warmed

As marzipan contains raw eggs in the finished mixture, care must be taken not to offer it to vulnerable people, i.e. the elderly or ill, pregnant women or babies, due to the risk of salmonella poisoning.

Use this very quick and easy to make marzipan to cover the top and sides of the cake before decorating with royal icing or adding glacé fruits. This quantity is enough to cover a 20 cm (8-inch) cake.

1. In a large bowl place the icing sugar, caster sugar and almonds; blend well.
2. Stir in the egg, almond essence and enough lemon juice to mix to a stiff dough. Form into a ball and knead lightly.
3. To apply the marzipan to the Christmas cake, trim the top of the cake, if necessary, since it is important to have a flat surface.
4. Measure around the side of the cake with a piece of string so you know how long to roll out the piece of marzipan to cover the side.
5. Take half the marzipan, knead gently, roll it out on a surface lightly dusted with icing sugar until it is as long as the string and as wide as the cake is deep.
6. Brush the side of the cake with the warmed apricot jam. Carefully lift the cake and place it side down at one end of the marzipan strip and then roll. Press the strip firmly onto the side of the cake, then flatten the join together.
7. Roll the remaining piece of marzipan into a circle to fit the top of the cake. Brush the top of the cake with the apricot jam and then turn the cake upside down onto the rolled-out marzipan and press down firmly.
8. Turn the cake the right way up and smooth the join where the top and sides meet.
9. Leave for at least 3 days to allow the marzipan to dry before covering with royal icing.

ROYAL ICING

PREPARATION TIME: 55 minutes +
overnight standing +
30 minutes to ice the cake

When icing a Christmas cake, I prefer to use a soft, flat royal icing. Although it takes time to make it, I think it's worth it for a special cake. This quantity is enough to cover a 20 cm (8-inch) cake. Glycerine can be found in the baking section of the supermarket, with the colourings and flavourings.

2 egg whites
450 g (1 lb) icing sugar, sieved
1 teaspoon glycerine

1. In a large, clean, grease-free bowl place the egg whites. Beat them with a fork hard enough to break up the albumen but without adding too many air bubbles.
2. Add half the icing sugar and, using a wooden spoon, stir to blend well. Beat for 5–10 minutes until the icing is glossy and smooth.
3. Cover the bowl with a clean, damp cloth and allow to stand for 30 minutes to allow any air bubbles to rise to the surface.
4. Gradually add the remaining icing sugar until the required consistency is achieved, then stir in the glycerine. For a flat icing, you can test whether the consistency is right by placing a wooden spoon in the centre of the mixture; it should fall slowly to the side. For rough icing, the mixture should be stiff enough for peaks to form when the icing is pulled up by the spoon.
5. If possible, the icing should now be placed in an airtight container and left overnight in a cool place.

TO FLAT ICE THE CAKE:
1. Place approximately 1 tablespoon of icing on the cake board and place the cake on top; remember to ensure it is in the centre of the board.
2. Spoon half the remaining icing mixture on the top of the cake and spread evenly over the top surface, using either a palette knife or a flat-bladed knife. Take an icing ruler or a palette knife longer than the diameter of the cake, draw it steadily across the top surface at an angle of 30°, to smooth the surface.
3. Leave the icing to dry for at least 6 hours before applying icing to the sides of the cake. Remember to cover the remaining icing to stop it drying out.
4. If you do not have an icing turntable, you may find it easier to ice the sides by placing the cake on a plate standing on the base of an upturned bowl. Spread the remaining icing on the sides of the cake and, with the palette knife, smooth it evenly round the sides. Holding the palette knife at an angle of 45°, draw it towards you to smooth the surface. Remove any excess icing carefully, to give a neat finish.
5. Allow the icing to dry for 24–48 hours before applying your choice of design to finish.

TO ROUGH ICE THE CAKE
1. Coat the cake with royal icing as described above, but icing the top and sides at the same time. While the icing is still soft, use the back of a spoon to draw the icing up into peaks over the top and sides.
2. Place your decorations in place before the icing sets.

MAKES 12–16 slices
PREPARATION TIME: 15–20 minutes
COOKING TIME: 1³/₄–2¹/₂ hours

MAKES 16–20 slices
PREPARATION TIME: 25–30 minutes
COOKING TIME: 2–2¹/₂ hours

DUNDEE CAKE

FRUIT & NUT CAKE

This fairly rich Scottish fruit cake, which is topped with almonds, is a time-honoured favourite.

The mixture of fruits, cherries, ginger and nuts gives this cake its unique flavour and appeal.

115 g (4 oz) raisins
115 g (4 oz) sultanas
115 g (4 oz) currants
50 g (2 oz) mixed peel, chopped
grated zest of 1 unwaxed lemon
175 g (6 oz) butter, softened
175 g (6 oz) caster sugar
3 eggs
sieve together: 225 g (8 oz) plain flour
   and **a pinch of salt**
   and **¹/₂ teaspoon baking powder**
   and **¹/₂ teaspoon ground mixed spice**
1 tablespoon sweet sherry
50 g (2 oz) whole blanched almonds

275 g (10 oz) butter, softened
275 g (10 oz) soft light brown sugar
5 eggs
sieve together: 175 g (6 oz) plain flour
   and **175 g (6 oz) wholemeal plain flour**
175 g (6 oz) raisins
115 g (4 oz) ready-to-eat dried apricots, chopped
115 g (4 oz) ready-to-eat dates, chopped
115 g (4 oz) glacé cherries, chopped
50 g (2 oz) mixed peel, chopped finely
80 g (3 oz) crystallised ginger, finely chopped
115 g (4 oz) brazil nuts, chopped
115 g (4 oz) pecan nuts, chopped
3–4 tablespoons sweet sherry

1. Mix together the raisins, sultanas, currants, mixed peel and lemon zest.
2. In a mixing bowl, cream together the butter and sugar until light in colour and fluffy. Beat in the eggs.
3. Fold in the flour, salt, baking powder and spice; mix well. Add the dried fruit and sherry and mix thoroughly.
4. Transfer the mixture to a greased and lined 18 cm (7-inch) round cake tin. Smooth the top and arrange the almonds in a circle around the top of the cake.
5. Bake at Gas Mark 3/electric oven 160°C/fan oven 140°C for 1³/₄–2¹/₂ hours or until a skewer inserted in the centre comes out clean.
6. Leave the cake in the tin for 15 minutes, then place on a wire rack to cool completely. To follow the Scottish tradition, present the cake with a tartan ribbon tied round its middle.

1. Cream together the butter and sugar until light in colour and fluffy. Beat in each egg.
2. Fold in the flours, mix well. Gradually combine the fruit and nuts and enough sherry to make a soft mixture.
3. Spoon the mixture into a greased and lined 23 cm (9-inch) round cake tin; smooth the top.
4. Bake at Gas Mark 3/electric oven 160°C/fan oven 140°C for 2–2¹/₂ hours until golden in colour and springy to the touch when a skewer inserted into the centre comes out clean.
5. Leave the cake to cool in the tin for 30 minutes before placing it on a wire rack to cool completely.

MAKES 16
PREPARATION TIME: 15–20 minutes
COOKING TIME: 20–25 minutes

MAKES 12–16 slices
PREPARATION TIME: 15–20minutes
COOKING TIME: 1¼–1½ hours

GIPSY CREAMS

JEWEL CAKE

No WI biscuit collection would be complete without this famous recipe, which has been featured on Channel 4's 'Countdown' programme.

50 g (2 oz) margarine, softened
50 g (2 oz) lard
50 g (2 oz) caster sugar
115 g (4 oz) self-raising flour, sieved
50 g (2 oz) rolled oats
1 tablespoon cocoa powder, sieved
2 tablespoons golden syrup, dissolved in 1 tablespoon hot water

FOR THE FILLING
25 g (1oz) butter
50 g (2 oz) icing sugar, sieved
1 tablespoon chocolate powder, sieved
a few drops of vanilla essence

1 Cream together the margarine, lard and sugar until light in colour and fluffy; then mix in all the other ingredients.
2 Roll the dough into balls the size of a large cherry. Place these on greased baking trays and flatten them with a fork which has been dipped in water; this stops the fork from sticking to the dough.
3 Bake at Gas Mark 4/electric oven 180°C/fan oven 160°C for 20–25 minutes until puffy and set. Leave them on trays to cool for 5 minutes before placing them on wire racks to cool completely.
4 To make the filling, cream the butter until soft. Gradually add the icing sugar and beat to a smooth consistency. Add the chocolate powder and vanilla essence and beat well.
5 When the biscuits are completely cold, sandwich them together with the filling.

The glacé cherries, dried fruit and nuts give this cake a jewelled appearance. It has a moist texture and fruity flavour.

175 g (6 oz) glacé cherries, halved
175 g (6 oz) sultanas
175 g (6 oz) raisins
25 g (1 oz) blanched almonds, chopped
25 g (1 oz) walnut pieces, chopped
115 g (4 oz) ready-to-eat dates, chopped
sieve together: 175 g (6 oz) plain flour
   and **a pinch of salt**
   and **1 teaspoon ground mixed spice**
50 g (2 oz) ground almonds
115 g (4 oz) butter, softened
115 g (4 oz) soft dark brown sugar
3 eggs
1 tablespoon sweet sherry

1 In a bowl, mix together the glacé cherries, sultanas, raisins, chopped nuts and dates.
2 Sift together the sieved flour mixture with the ground almonds.
3 In a large mixing bowl, cream the butter and the sugar until light in colour and fluffy. Beat in each egg.
4 Fold in the flour and almond mixture, and then stir in the fruit and the sherry.
5 Spoon the mixture into a greased and lined 18 cm (7-inch) round cake tin.
6 Bake at Gas Mark 3/electric oven 170°C/fan oven 150°C for 1¼–1½ hours until dark golden in colour, and a skewer inserted in the centre comes out clean.
7 Leave to cool in the tin for 15 minutes before turning out on to a wire rack to cool completely.

MAKES 24
PREPARATION TIME: 10–15 minutes
COOKING TIME: 16–20 minutes

These are small, soft fruit biscuits.

115 g (4 oz) butter, softened
80 g (3 oz) caster sugar
1 egg, separated
sieve together: 200 g (7 oz) plain flour
    and a pinch of salt
    and 1/2 teaspoon ground mixed spice
    and 1/2 teaspoon ground cinnamon
50 g (2 oz) currants
25 g (1oz) mixed peel, chopped
1–2 tablespoons milk
a little caster sugar

EASTER BISCUITS

1 In a bowl, cream together the butter and sugar until light and fluffy. Beat in the egg yolk.
2 Fold the flour, salt and spices into the mixture, with the currants and peel. Add enough milk to give a soft dough.
3 Lightly knead the dough on a floured surface and roll out to 5 mm (1/4 inch) thick. Cut out, using a 6 cm (2 1/2-inch) fluted cutter. Place the biscuits on greased baking trays.
4 Bake at Gas Mark 6/electric oven 200°C/fan oven 180°C for 8–10 minutes, then brush with egg white and sprinkle with caster sugar. Return to the oven for a further 8–10 minutes.
5 Allow the biscuits to cool for a few minutes before placing them on wire racks to cool completely.

MAKES 20–24
PREPARATION TIME: 10–15 minutes
COOKING TIME: 15–25 minutes

These small light but rich cakes, which are usually baked in paper cases.

175 g (6 oz) butter, softened
175 g (6 oz) caster sugar
3 eggs
175 g (6 oz) self-raising flour, sieved

QUEEN'S CAKES

1 In a bowl, cream the butter and sugar together until light and fluffy. Add the eggs, beating well.
2 Fold in the flour and mix well.
3 Divide the mixture evenly between 20–24 paper cases, and place them on baking trays.
4 Bake at Gas Mark 5/electric oven 190°C/fan oven 170°C for 15–25 minutes until well risen and golden in colour.
5 Allow the cakes to stand for 5 minutes before transferring them to wire racks to cool immediately.

VARIATIONS
Add one of the following after the flour, stirring in gently.
80 g (3 oz) glacé cherries, chopped
80 g (3 oz) chocolate chips
80 g (3 oz) sultanas

MAKES 12–16 slices
PREPARATION TIME: 20–25 minutes
COOKING TIME: 1–1 1/2 hours

This cake, which has an unusual combination of chocolate and apricot, has a light, moist texture. I use a home-made jam with lovely chunks of fruit.

225 g (8 oz) butter, softened
225 g (8 oz) caster sugar
5 eggs, separated
1 tablespoon apricot jam
175 g (6 oz) plain chocolate, melted and cooled
sieve together: 225 g (8 oz) plain flour
    and 2 teaspoons baking powder
50 g (2 oz) ground almonds

CHOCOLATE & APRICOT JAM CAKE

1 Cream together the butter and sugar in a large bowl until light and fluffy. Beat in the egg yolks and the apricot jam.
2 Stir the melted and cooled chocolate into the creamed mixture.
3 Fold in the flour, baking powder and ground almonds.
4 In a clean grease-free bowl, whisk the egg whites until firm. Fold in carefully to the cake mixture.
5 Spoon the mixture into a greased and lined 23 cm (9-inch) round cake tin; smooth the top.
6 Bake at Gas Mark 3/electric oven 170°C/fan oven 150°C for 1–1 1/2 hours until set and a skewer inserted in the centre comes out clean.
7 Leave the cake in the tin to cool completely.

MAKES 10–12 slices
PREPARATION TIME: 20–25 minutes
COOKING TIME: 40–50 minutes

This very light-textured cake is ideal for lunch boxes.

140 g (4½ oz) butter, softened
150 g (5 oz) icing sugar, sieved
2 eggs
sieve together: 140 g (4½ oz) plain flour
    and 1 teaspoon baking powder
    and a large pinch bicarbonate of soda
100 ml (3½ fl oz) full-fat milk
50 g (2 oz) brazil nuts, chopped finely
3 tablespoons clear honey
65 g (2½ oz) polenta

HONEY, NUT & POLENTA CAKE

1 Cream the butter and icing sugar together until light in colour and fluffy. Beat in the eggs.
2 Fold in the flour, baking powder and bicarbonate of soda. Stir in the milk. Stir in the nuts, honey and polenta, mixing well.
3 Spoon the mixture into a lightly greased and floured 20 cm (8-inch) tube tin.
4 Bake at Gas Mark 5/electric oven 190°C/fan oven 170°C for 40–50 minutes until pale golden in colour, firm to the touch and a skewer inserted in the centre of the cake comes out clean.
5 Leave the cake in the tin for 15 minutes before turning it onto a wire rack to cool completely.
6 Wrap tightly in foil and leave for 2 days before serving.

MAKES 12–16 slices
PREPARATION TIME: 20–30 minutes
COOKING TIME: 1¼–1¾ hours

225 g (8 oz) butter, softened
225 g (8 oz) soft light brown sugar
4 eggs, separated
finely grated zest and juice
    of 1 unwaxed lemon
sieve together: 175 g (6 oz) wholemeal
    self-raising flour
    and 5 ml (1 teaspoon) baking powder
50 g (2 oz) ground almonds
115 g (4 oz) walnut pieces, chopped
350 g (12 oz) carrots, peeled and grated

PASSION CAKE

1 Cream the butter and sugar together in a bowl until light in colour and fluffy.
2 Beat in the egg yolks, then stir in the lemon zest and juice.
3 Fold in the flour and baking powder; stir in the ground almonds and the walnuts.
4 In a clean, grease-free bowl, whisk the egg whites until stiff; fold them into the cake mixture with the carrots, mixing thoroughly.
5 Spoon the mixture into a greased and lined 20 cm (8-inch) round cake tin; with the back of a spoon smooth the top and hollow the centre slightly.
6 Bake at Gas Mark 4/electric oven 180°C/fan oven 160°C for 1¼–1¾ hours until the cake is firm to the touch and golden in colour. Leave the cake to cool slightly in the tin, and then turn onto a rack to cool completely.
7 To make the icing, place all the icing ingredients, except the walnut halves, in a bowl and beat together until smooth.
8 When it is cold, cut the cake in half, spread half the icing on one side, sandwich together and spread the remaining icing over the top and sides of the cake. Decorate the top with walnut halves.

This is also familiarly known as Carrot Cake. The carrots produce sweetness and moisture and the tangy topping complements the sweetness.

FOR THE TOPPING
50 g (2 oz) butter, softened
225 g (8 oz) icing sugar
115 g (4 oz) low-fat cream cheese
3 tablespoons lemon curd
1 teaspoon lemon juice
50 g (2 oz) walnut halves

This is the quickest and easiest way of preparing all types of cakes.

As all the ingredients are beaten together, air is incorporated into the mixture to form air cells, which are stabilised by the sugar which provides a structure around them. By using a softened fat (page 6), which should be taken from the refrigerator a short time before it is required, very little beating will be required to combine all the ingredients of sugar, eggs and flour. Additional raising agent is required, however, as sufficient air is not introduced during the mixing process.

THE ALL-IN-ONE-METHOD

During baking, the fat melts, the raising agent reacts with the liquid from the added egg to produce carbon dioxide and steam. As pressure builds up inside the cake, these gases transfer to the air cells formed during the mixing and allow the cake to rise. By the end of baking, this movement ceases as the proteins in the flour and eggs are set.

The cooked cake consists of a large number of air cells surrounded by a network of proteins in which starch granules are held. The texture of a cake made by using the all-in-one method is fairly open.

PROBLEMS THAT CAN OCCUR WITH CAKES MADE BY THE ALL-IN-ONE METHOD, AND REMEDIES

HOLLOW TOP
- Fat allowed to become too soft at the start: use straight from the refrigerator.
- Mixture overbeaten: beat for less time.
- Too cool an oven: adjust temperature.
- Insufficient cooking: adjust cooking time.

DOMED TOP
- Oven temperature too high: adjust temperature.
- Cake baked too high in oven: adjust shelf position.

CLOSE, DAMP TEXTURE
- Mixture too slack before cooking, caused by too much liquid, too little flour or too much sugar: check proportions.
- Oven temperature too low: adjust temperature.
- Insufficient cooking: adjust cooking time.

RISEN UNEVENLY
- Mixture spread unevenly in tin: ensure mixture is spread evenly.
- Tin warped during cooking: buy a heavier gauge of tin.
- Oven shelves not level: adjust using a spirit level.

COLLAR ON EDGE OF BAKED CAKE
- Too much raising agent: check proportions.
- Fan oven preheated: place cake in cold fan oven.
- Cake has risen too rapidly and sunk, caused by cake being baked too high in oven: adjust shelf position.

COARSE TEXTURE
- Too much raising agent: check proportions.

MAKES 12–16 slices
PREPARATION TIME: 10 minutes
COOKING TIME: 40–50 minutes

ALL-IN-ONE COFFEE CAKE

This cake is delicious plain or covered with coffee buttercream icing.

175 g (6 oz) margarine or butter, softened
175 g (6 oz) caster sugar
sieve together: 175 g (6 oz) self-raising flour
    and **1 teaspoon baking powder**
2 tablespoons instant coffee powder
    dissolved in 1 tablespoon hot water
3 eggs

1 Place all the ingredients in a large bowl. Beat together until well mixed for 3 minutes with a wooden spoon or 1 minute with an electric mixer.
2 Place the mixture in a greased and lined 20 cm (8-inch) round cake tin.
3 Bake at Gas Mark 4/electric oven 180°C/fan oven 160°C for 40–50 minutes until the cake is springy to the touch and dark golden in colour.
4 Allow the cake to cool in the tin for 10 minutes before placing it on a wire rack to cool completely.

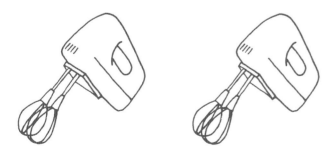

MAKES 8–12 slices
PREPARATION TIME: 5–6 minutes
COOKING TIME: 20–30 minutes

ALL-IN-ONE VICTORIA SANDWICH

Here, I have transformed the traditional recipe (page 32) into a quick and easy modern form. Remember to use soft tub margarine straight from the refrigerator.

175 g (6 oz) soft margarine or butter, softened
175 g (6 oz) caster sugar
sieve together: 175 g (6 oz) self-raising flour
    and **1 teaspoon baking powder**
3 eggs

FOR THE FILLING
6 tablespoons raspberry jam

1 Place all ingredients in a bowl. Beat together with a wooden spoon for 3 minutes or with an electric mixer for 1 minute.
2 Grease and base line two 18 cm (7-inch) sandwich tins. Divide the mixture equally between the tins, and level their tops.
3 Bake at Gas Mark 4/electric oven 180°C/fan oven 160°C for 20–30 minutes until golden brown and springy to the touch.
4 Allow the cakes to cool in the tin for 10 minutes before placing them onto a wire rack to cool completely.
5 When cold, sandwich the two halves together with raspberry jam. Dust the top of the cake with caster sugar.

CHOCOLATE ALL-IN-ONE VICTORIA SANDWICH: Mix together to a paste 2 tablespoons cocoa powder and 3 tablespoons boiling water. Allow the paste to cool then stir gently it into the main mixture.

LEMON ALL-IN-ONE VICTORIA SANDWICH: Stir the grated zest and juice of an unwaxed lemon into the main mixture. When cooked, sandwich together with lemon curd.

MAKES 16–20 slices
PREPARATION TIME: 25 minutes
COOKING TIME: 50–70 minutes

CARROT, WALNUT & CINNAMON CAKE

This is a particularly moist cake with a wonderful spicy flavour.

225 g (8 oz) butter, softened
225 g (8 oz) soft dark brown sugar
4 eggs
sieve together: 100 g (3½ oz) self-raising flour
    and **100 g (3½ oz) wholemeal self-raising flour**
    and **1 teaspoon baking powder**
    and **2 teaspoons ground cinnamon**
25 g (1 oz) ground almonds
275 g (10 oz) carrots, peeled and grated coarsely
100 g (3½ oz) walnut pieces, chopped coarsely
grated zest and juice of an unwaxed orange

1 Place the butter, sugar, eggs, flours, baking powder, ground cinnamon and ground almonds in a large mixing bowl and beat with a wooden spoon for 3 minutes or with an electric mixer for 1 minute.
2 Stir in the carrots, walnuts and the orange juice and zest.
3 Spoon the mixture into a greased and lined 23 cm (9-inch) round cake tin.
4 Bake at Gas Mark 4/electric oven 180°C/fan oven 160°C for 50–70 minutes until the cake is golden in colour and a skewer inserted into the centre comes out clean.
5 Remove the cake from the oven and leave to cool in the tin for 15 minutes before placing it on a wire rack to cool completely.

MAKES approximately 24
PREPARATION TIME: 25 minutes + 1 hour chilling time
COOKING TIME: 15–20 minutes

CHOCOLATE COOKIES

These are gently flavoured chocolate cookies which freeze well.

sieve together: 150 g (5 oz) plain flour
    and **50 g (2 oz) cocoa powder**
    and **½ teaspoon bicarbonate of soda**
50 g (2 oz) soft light brown sugar
50 g (2 oz) caster sugar
115 g (4 oz) butter, softened
1 teaspoon almond essence
1 egg white

1 In a bowl, place the flour, cocoa powder, bicarbonate of soda and sugars; blend well.
2 Beat the butter until creamy, add the flour mixture and the remaining ingredients, and beat to form a soft dough.
3 Knead gently on a lightly floured board, and then shape it into a long log. Wrap in greaseproof paper and chill in the refrigerator for at least 1 hour.
4 Remove the dough from the refrigerator, cut it into slices 5 mm (¼ inch) thick. Place these on greased baking sheets, remembering to allow for spreading.
5 Bake at Gas Mark 4/electric oven 180°C/fan oven 160°C for 15–20 minutes until they are puffy and set.
6 Remove them from the oven and allow to cool on the trays for a few minutes before transferring them to a wire rack to cool completely.

CAPPUCCINO BARS *pictured opposite*

MAKES 12–16 bars
PREPARATION TIME: 15 minutes
COOKING TIME: 35–45 minutes

2 tablespoons coffee concentrate
1 tablespoon cocoa powder
225 g (8 oz) butter, softened
225 g (8 oz) caster sugar
4 eggs
sieve together: 225 g (8 oz) self-raising flour
and 1 teaspoon baking powder

FOR THE FROSTING
115 g (4 oz) milk chocolate
50 g (2 oz) butter, softened
3 tablespoons milk
175 g (6 oz) icing sugar, sieved

These chocolate bars with coffee flavouring are enhanced by the milk chocolate icing.

1. In a large bowl, blend together the coffee liquid and the cocoa powder. Add all the remaining cake ingredients and, using a wooden spoon, mix together until well combined; this should take about 2–3 minutes. It is important not to overbeat the mixture.
2. Spoon the mixture into a shallow (4 cm/1½ inches) greased and lined 18 x 28 cm (7- x 11-inch) tin; smooth the top.
3. Bake at Gas Mark 4/electric oven 180°C/fan oven 160°C for 35–45 minutes until well risen and firm to the touch. Cool in the tin for 10 minutes, and then turn out onto a wire rack to cool completely.
4. To make the frosting, melt the chocolate, butter and milk in a bowl over a pan of simmering water. Remove the bowl from the heat; beat in the icing sugar until smooth. When cold spread over the top of the cake, and cut the cake into bars.

BISCOTTI

MAKES 14
PREPARATION TIME: 20 minutes
COOKING TIME: 25–35 minutes

sieve together: 275 g (10 oz) plain flour
and 1 teaspoon baking powder
150 g (5 oz) caster sugar
2 whole eggs, plus 1 egg yolk
1 teaspoon vanilla essence
115 g (4 oz) whole blanched almonds
icing sugar, to dust (optional)

These are crisp, dry Italian cookies that look a bit like slices of toasted bread. They are delicious when dipped in coffee.

1. Place the flour, baking powder, sugar, eggs and egg yolk, vanilla essence and almonds in a bowl.
2. Using a wooden spoon, mix the ingredients together until the mixture forms a soft dough. Knead the dough gently on a lightly floured surface until it is smooth.
3. Shape the dough into a log and place on a greased baking sheet, then flatten to a thickness of 2.5 cm (1 inch). Dust the top with flour.
4. With a sharp knife, cut two-thirds through the dough to make 14 slices.
5. Bake at Gas Mark 4/electric oven 180°C/fan oven 160°C for 15–20 minutes until light golden and firm. Remove from the oven and, while still warm, completely cut through the biscotti to make individual slices.
6. Place the slices cut side up on a baking sheet. Return to the oven and continue baking for 10–15 minutes until golden.
7. Cool the biscotti on a wire rack. If required, dust with icing sugar.

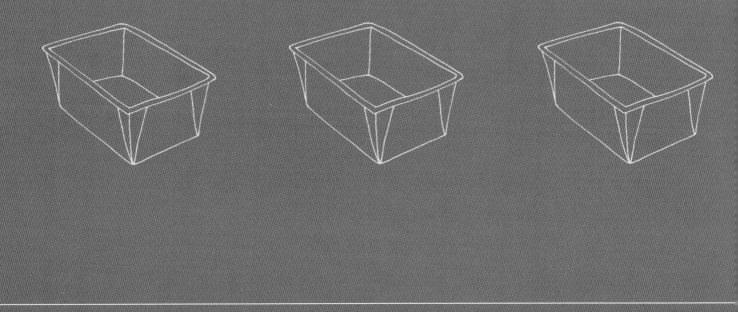

THE RUBBING-IN METHOD

This method is used for cakes, which are usually made with half, or less than half, fat to flour. The fat — which should be used straight out of the refrigerator — is cut into fairly small pieces and rubbed lightly into the flour with the fingertips and thumbs. At the same time, the mixture should be lifted well above the bowl to help incorporate air into the cake; continue until the mixture resembles fine breadcrumbs. The texture of a cake made by the rubbed-in method is fairly open.

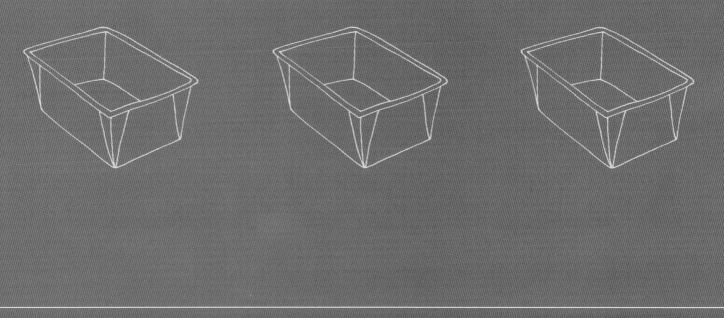

PROBLEMS THAT CAN OCCUR WITH CAKES MADE BY THE RUBBING-IN METHOD, AND REMEDIES

LARGE PEAK IN CENTRE OR TOP BADLY CRACKED
- Oven too hot: adjust temperature.
- Cake placed too near top of oven: adjust shelf position.

CAKE SUNK IN CENTRE
- Mixture too slack before cooking, caused by too much liquid, too little flour or too much sugar: check proportions.
- Oven too cool: adjust temperature.

FRUIT SUNK TO THE BOTTOM OF THE CAKE
- Fruit not dried properly after washing: always ensure fruit is dried.
- Mixture too slack before cooking caused by too much liquid: adjust proportions.
- Oven too cool: adjust temperature.

RASPBERRY BUNS *pictured opposite*

MAKES 10
PREPARATION TIME: 10–15 minutes
COOKING TIME: 15–20 minutes

sieve together: 225 g (8 oz) self-raising flour
and a pinch of salt
80 g (3 oz) margarine, chilled
80 g (3 oz) caster sugar
2 eggs
raspberry jam

I remember learning to make these at school, and because they are quick and easy to prepare, they are great for children to make. They are best eaten fresh – not difficult when children are around.

1 Place the flour and salt into a mixing bowl and rub in the margarine until the mixture resembles fine breadcrumbs. Stir in the sugar.
2 Make a well in the centre of the mixture, add the eggs and mix well to form a stiff dough.
3 Turn the dough onto a lightly floured surface and form it into a roll. Cut the roll into 10 pieces and shape each into a ball.
4 Place the balls onto a lightly greased baking tray, ensuring there is space between each.
5 Make a hole in the middle of each ball and fill with a little raspberry jam; close the hole carefully and dust the tops with a little sugar.
6 Bake at Gas Mark 6/electric oven 200°C/fan oven 180°C for 15–20 minutes until the buns are golden-brown. Leave to cool on the tray for 5 minutes before transferring them on a wire rack to cool completely.
7 The buns will keep fresh if stored in an airtight container for 2–3 days.

PLUM & WALNUT CAKE

MAKES 12–16 slices
PREPARATION TIME:
fruit 75 minutes +10 minutes
COOKING TIME: 45–60 minutes

450 g (1lb) plums, quartered and stoned
sieve together: 225 g (8 oz) plain flour
and 1 1/2 teaspoons baking powder
and 1/2 teaspoon bicarbonate of soda
and 1 teaspoon ground cinnamon
50 g (2 oz) butter, chilled
175 g (6 oz) granulated sugar
2 eggs, beaten
juice and grated zest of 1 unwaxed lemon
50 g (2 oz) walnut pieces, roughly chopped

Plums and walnuts are one of my favourite combinations and this cake should prove a hit. The best flavour will be achieved using Victoria plums but other varieties can be used.

1 Place the plums in a saucepan and, over a very gentle heat, poach them for 15 minutes. Do not add any additional liquid and remember to stir occasionally. Allow to cool for 30 minutes.
2 Place the flour in a bowl with the baking powder and bicarbonate of soda and the cinnamon. Rub in the butter until it resembles fine breadcrumbs, and stir in the sugar.
3 Gradually add the eggs, juice and the zest of the lemon until a soft mixture has formed.
4 Stir in the walnuts and the cold plums. Mix well.
5 Place the mixture in a greased and lined 20 cm (8-inch) round cake tin; smooth the top.
6 Bake at Gas Mark 3/electric oven 170°C/fan oven 150°C for 45–60 minutes until golden-brown in colour and springy to the touch.
7 Leave the cake in the tin for 10 minutes before placing it on a wire rack to cool completely.

FOR THE PASTRY
350 g (12 oz) plain flour, sieved
175 g (6 oz) butter, chilled
water to mix

FOR THE FILLING
450 g (1 lb) raisins
450 g (1 lb) currants
80 g (3 oz) blanched almonds, chopped
115 g (4 oz) mixed peel, chopped finely
50 g (2 oz) soft dark brown sugar
sieve together: 225 g (8 oz) plain flour
    and 1 teaspoon ground nutmeg
    and 1 teaspoon ground ginger
    and 1 teaspoon ground cinnamon
3 eggs
2 tablespoons whisky

MAKES 12–16 slices
PREPARATION TIME: 10–15 minutes
COOKING TIME: 1¼–1½ hours

Children love this light fruit cake so it is ideal for lunch boxes.

sieve together: 225 g (8 oz) plain flour
    and 1 teaspoon baking powder
115 g (4 oz) butter, chilled
115 g (4 oz) caster sugar
225 g (8 oz) mixed dried fruit
2 eggs, beaten
4 tablespoons milk

SERVES 20
PREPARATION TIME: 1 hour
COOKING TIME: 2¼–3 hours

This is a traditional Scottish cake. It consists of a pastry case around a spice- and whisky-flavoured fruit filling. It is served cold with a nip of whisky at Hogmanay celebrations.

BLACK BUN

SEMI-RICH FRUIT CAKE

1 To make the pastry, place the flour in a bowl and rub in the butter until the mixture resembles fine breadcrumbs. Add enough water to form a stiff dough.
2 Roll out the pastry thinly and use two-thirds to line an 18 cm (7-inch) square cake tin. The remaining one-third will form the lid.
3 To make the filling, place the raisins, currants, almonds, peel, sugar, flour and spices in a large bowl; mix well.
4 Beat together the eggs and the whisky. Stir this mixture into the dry ingredients to bind. If it seems too dry, add a further 1–2 tablespoons whisky.
5 Place the mixture in the pastry-lined tin, pressing the mixture down firmly.
6 Form a pastry lid from the remaining pastry, moisten the edges of the lid and place over the top of the filling; seal well. Using a long thin skewer, pierce the top several times, ensuring that you go through to the bottom of the pastry at the bottom of the pan to stop the pastry puckering up and causing air pockets.
7 Bake at Gas Mark 3/electric oven 160°C/fan oven 140°C for 2½–3 hours until pale golden in colour.
8 Leave the cake in the tin for 30 minutes before turning it out onto a wire rack to cool completely.

1 Put the flour and baking powder into a bowl, and rub the butter into them until the mixture resembles fine breadcrumbs.
2 Add the sugar, the mixed fruit, eggs and enough milk to give a soft dropping consistency.
3 Put the mixture into a greased and lined 18 cm (7-inch) round cake tin.
4 Bake at Gas Mark 3/electric oven 160°C/fan oven 140°F for 1¼–1½ hours until pale golden in colour, and firm to the touch.
5 Leave to cool in tin for 10 minutes before placing on wire rack to cool completely.

MAKES 10–12 slices
PREPARATION TIME: 20–25 minutes
COOKING TIME: 50–70 minutes

This cake, which has a good combination of flavours, is ideal to take on picnics.

sieve together: 150 g (5 oz) self-raising flour
   and 115 g (4 oz) wholemeal self–raising flour
115 g (4 oz) soft light brown sugar
115 g (4 oz) butter, chilled
175 g (6 oz) ready-to-eat dates, chopped finely
zest and juice of 2 unwaxed oranges
3 eggs

ORANGE & DATE LOAF

1 In a bowl, mix the flours and sugar. Rub in the butter until it resembles fine breadcrumbs.
2 Stir in the dates and the zest of the oranges.
3 Mix together the orange juice and the eggs, then add them to the dry ingredients to give a soft mixture.
4 Place the mixture in a greased and lined 900 g (2 lb) loaf tin.
5 Bake at Gas Mark 4/electric oven 180°C/fan oven 160°C for 50–70 minutes until the cake is light golden in colour and firm to the touch.
6 Leave the cake in the tin for 15 minutes to cool, and then place it onto a wire rack to cool completely.

MAKES 24
PREPARATION TIME: 10 minutes
COOKING TIME: 15–25 minutes

These delicately cardamom-flavoured cookies will quickly become favourites.

sieve together: 80 g (3 oz) icing sugar
   and 225 g (8 oz) plain flour
a pinch of salt
20 cardamom pods, seeds removed and crushed (page 18)
225 g (8 oz) butter, chilled
80 g (3 oz) blanched almonds, finely chopped
$\frac{1}{2}$ teaspoon almond essence
25 g (1 oz) blanched almonds, roughly chopped

CARDAMOM & ALMOND COOKIES

1 In a bowl, place the icing sugar, flour, salt and crushed cardamom seeds. Rub the butter into the flour mixture until a dough is formed.
2 Work in the chopped almonds and essence.
3 Divide the mixture into 24 balls which should then be placed well apart on lightly greased baking sheets.
4 With the palm of the hand, flatten each ball slightly, then sprinkle with the roughly chopped almonds.
5 Bake at Gas Mark 4/electric oven 180°C/fan oven 160°C for 15–20 minutes until the cookies are golden in colour.
6 Allow the cookies to cool on the trays for 5 minutes before transferring them to a wire rack to cool completely.
7 They will stay fresh stored in a airtight container for up to 1 week.

MAKES 10–12 slices
PREPARATION TIME: 25 minutes
COOKING TIME: 50–60 minutes

This cake would be ideal as a lighter alternative to Simnel Cake (page 36), and is very useful as an afternoon tea-loaf.

sieve together:
   115 g (4 oz) wholemeal self-raising flour
   and 115 g (4 oz) self-raising flour
115 g (4 oz) butter, chilled
85 g (3 oz) soft dark brown sugar
115 g (4 oz) marzipan, cut into cubes
2 eggs
200 g (7 oz) mincemeat
2 tablespoons demerara sugar

MINCEMEAT & MARZIPAN LOAF

1 Place the flours in a bowl, add the butter and rub it into the flour until a fine breadcrumb texture is formed.
2 Stir in the sugar and marzipan; mix well.
3 Beat the eggs together, then add them with the mincemeat to the dry ingredients. Combine evenly.
4 Spoon the mixture into a greased and lined 900 g (2 lb) loaf tin, smooth the top. Sprinkle the top with demerara sugar.
5 Bake at Gas Mark 4/electric oven 180°C/fan oven 160°C for 50–60 minutes until the cake is golden-brown and well risen.
6 Let the cake cool in the tin for 15 minutes before placing it on a wire rack to cool completely.

MAKES 12–16 slices
PREPARATION TIME: 5 minutes +
overnight soaking + 20 minutes
COOKING TIME: 50–60 minutes

This moist apple cake has a **delicious date filling** sandwiched between the cake and almond topping.

FOR THE FILLING
350 g (12 oz) ready-to-eat dates, chopped
80 g (3 oz) caster sugar
150 ml (5 fl oz) water
80 ml (3 fl oz) sweet Madeira

FOR THE ALMOND TOPPING
80 g (3 oz) self-raising flour, sieved
25 g (1oz) butter, chilled
80 g (3 oz) demerara sugar
50 g (2 oz) flaked almonds

FOR THE CAKE
sieve together: 80 g (3 oz) self-raising flour
and $\frac{1}{2}$ teaspoon baking powder
50 g (2 oz) butter, chilled
25 g (1 oz) ground almonds
50 g (2 oz) caster sugar
1 large egg
2 tablespoons milk
1 small eating apple, cored and diced

1 To prepare the filling, place the chopped dates, sugar and water in a small saucepan and simmer gently for 15 minutes. Stir in the Madeira and leave until cold or, if possible, overnight.

2 To make the topping, place the flour in a bowl, rub in the butter until a breadcrumb-like mixture is achieved, stir in the sugar and flaked almonds. Next stir in 2 tablespoons of water to form a coarse, lumpy mixture; leave to one side.

3 To make the cake, place the flour and baking powder in a large bowl, add the remaining ingredients and beat until smooth.

4 Spoon the cake mixture into a greased and lined 20 cm (8-inch) round cake tin.

5 Spread the date mixture over the cake mixture, then sprinkle the almond topping evenly over the top.

6 Bake at Gas Mark 4/electric oven 180°C/fan oven 160°C for 50–60 minutes until the cake is firm and golden in colour. Leave it in the tin to cool completely.

DATE, APPLE & MADEIRA CAKE

MAKES 12–16 slices
PREPARATION TIME: 15–20 minutes
COOKING TIME: 1–1½ hours

MAKES 12–16 slices
PREPARATION TIME: 15–20 minutes
COOKING TIME: 35–45 minutes

RICOTTA CINNAMON CAKE

GINGER & WALNUT CAKE

Ricotta is a fragrant Italian cheese made from ewe's milk whey. Do not drain the liquid from around the cheese before using it in the recipe.

Ginger, walnuts, honey and golden syrup gives this cake a moist yet crunchy texture; the honey and walnut topping continues the flavours.

sieve together: 225 g (8 oz) self-raising flour
    and a pinch of salt and 1 teaspoon baking powder
115 g (4 oz) caster sugar
80 g (3 oz) butter, chilled
2 eggs
115 g (4 oz) ricotta cheese
150 ml (5 fl oz) milk
1 tablespoon apricot jam

FOR THE TOPPING
50 g (2 oz) plain flour, sieved
50 g (2 oz) soft dark brown sugar
1½ teaspoons ground cinnamon
25 g (1 oz) butter, chilled

1   Place the flour, salt, baking powder and sugar in a bowl. Rub in the butter until the mixture resembles fine breadcrumbs.
2   Beat together the eggs, cheese, milk and jam.
3   Stir this mixture into the dry ingredients and beat to form a smooth batter.
4   Spoon into a greased and lined 20 cm (8-inch) round cake tin.
5   To make topping, place the flour, sugar and cinnamon in a bowl, and rub in the butter. Spoon this over the cake mixture in the tin.
6   Bake at Gas Mark 4/electric oven 180°C/fan oven 160°C for 1–1½ hours until the cake is golden in colour, and firm and springy to the touch.
7   Leave the cake in the tin for 10 minutes before removing it to a wire rack to cool completely.
8   This cake should be eaten within 5 days and will keep best if stored in an airtight container.

sieve together: 225 g (8 oz) self-raising flour
    and 1 teaspoon baking powder
    and 1 tablespoon ground ginger
175 g (6 oz) butter, chilled
8 tablespoons clear honey
8 tablespoons golden syrup
115 g (4 oz) soft light brown sugar
4 eggs, beaten
115 g (4 oz) walnut pieces, roughly chopped
80 g (3 oz) crystallised ginger, chopped

FOR THE TOPPING
175 g (6 oz) icing sugar, sieved
85 g (3 oz) butter, softened
2 tablespoons clear honey
walnut halves

1   Place the flour, baking powder and ginger in a bowl. Rub the butter into the flour mixture until it resembles fine breadcrumbs.
2   Beat in the honey, syrup, sugar and eggs; mix well.
3   Stir the walnuts and ginger into the mixture.
4   Divide the mixture between two greased and lined 20 cm (8-inch) sandwich cake tins.
5   Bake at Gas Mark 3/electric oven 170°C/fan oven 150°C for 35–45 minutes until golden, and firm and springy to the touch.
6   Cool the two cake halves in the tins for 10 minutes before turning them out onto wire racks to cool completely.
7   To make the topping, place the icing sugar in a bowl, beat in the butter and honey to form a soft icing. Spread this in the centre and on top of the cake. Decorate the top with walnut halves.

MAKES 12–16 slices
PREPARATION TIME: 20 minutes
COOKING TIME: 35–45 minutes

WENSLEYDALE APPLE CAKE

The apples and cheese produce an unusual cake, **ideal for teatime or for supper.** I prefer to use Cox's apples but any crisp dessert apple will produce good results.

225 g (8 oz) self-raising flour, sieved
115 g (4 oz) caster sugar
115 g (4 oz) butter, chilled
1 egg
4 tablespoons milk
3 medium-sized apples, peeled, cored and sliced
150 g (5 oz) Wensleydale cheese, grated coarsely

FOR THE TOPPING
25 g (1 oz) caster sugar
1 teaspoon ground cinnamon
50 g (2 oz) butter, chilled

1 Place the flour in a bowl, add the sugar and rub in the butter until the mixture resembles fine breadcrumbs.
2 Add the egg and milk, and mix to a soft dough.
3 Spread half the mixture into a well-greased and lined 20 cm (8-inch) round cake tin. Arrange half the apple slices on top.
4 Spread the remaining mixture over the layer of apple; smooth the top.
5 Arrange the remaining apple slices on top, and sprinkle over the cheese.
6 For the topping, sprinkle with sugar and cinnamon, and dot with butter.
7 Bake at Gas Mark 5/electric oven 190°C/fan oven 170°C for 35–45 minutes until the top of the cake is dark golden and firm to the touch
8 Leave the cake in the tin to cool for 20 minutes before turning it out onto a wire rack to cool completely.

MAKES 12–16 slices
PREPARATION TIME: 25–30 minutes
COOKING TIME: 1–1½ hours

APPLE & RAISIN CAKE

The sugar topping gives a crunchy finish to this tasty cake.
I prefer to use Bramley apples for this cake.

sieve together: 350 g (12 oz) self-raising flour
    and 1 teaspoon baking powder
150 g (5 oz) butter, chilled
150 g (5 oz) soft light brown sugar
350 g (12 oz) cooking apples
25 g (1oz) demerara sugar
½ teaspoon ground nutmeg
115 g (4 oz) raisins
2 eggs
125 ml (4 fl oz) milk

FOR THE TOPPING
25 g (1 oz) demerara sugar

1 In a large bowl, place the flour and baking powder. Rub the butter into the flour until the mixture resembles fine breadcrumbs and stir in the soft light brown sugar.
2 Peel, core and thinly slice the apples, coat in demerara sugar and nutmeg; add to the dry ingredients. Stir in the raisins.
3 Stir in the eggs and enough milk to form a soft dropping dough.
4 Place the dough in a greased and base-lined 20 cm (8-inch) round cake tin. Sprinkle the top with demerara sugar.
5 Bake at Gas Mark 4/electric oven 180°C/fan oven 160°C for 1–1½ hours until the cake is golden in colour and firm to the touch.
6 Leave the cake to cool in the tin for 15 minutes before turning it onto a wire rack to cool completely.

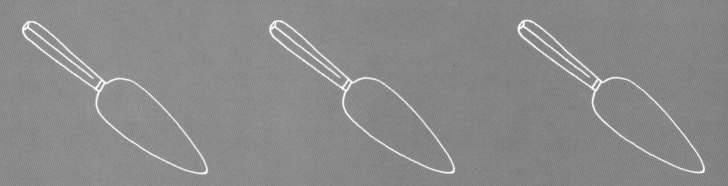

This is a very easy method of preparing cakes since a minimum amount of handling is required. It is the traditional method for preparing cakes of the gingerbread variety. Some fruit cakes are also made by the melting method.

THE MELTING METHOD

The fat, sugar, syrup, and fruit (if used) are heated gently until melted. The mixture is cooled and added to the dry ingredients and then beaten together with the egg until well mixed. The texture of gingerbread is fairly open and that of a fruit cake fairly crumbly but both are moist.

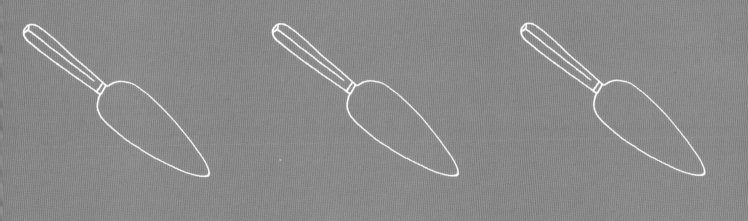

PROBLEMS THAT CAN OCCUR WITH CAKES MADE BY THE MELTING METHOD, AND REMEDIES

CAKE SUNK IN CENTRE
- Too much raising agent added: check proportions.
- Too much syrup added: take care when measuring out.
- Oven temperature too high: adjust temperature.
- Cake baked too high in oven: adjust shelf position.

SHINY TOP & CLOSED TEXTURED
- Mixture overbeaten: gently stir and do not beat a melted mixture.

CRACKED ON TOP & RATHER DRY
- Not enough liquid added: check proportions.
- Oven temperature too high: adjust temperature.
- Cake baked too high in oven: adjust shelf position

MAKES 12–16 slices
PREPARATION TIME; 20–25 minutes
COOKING TIME: 30–40 minutes

CHOCOLATE & CINNAMON MOUSSE CAKE

You must not worry if this moist mousse-like cake sinks. It is delicious eaten warm with ice cream. For the most intense chocolate flavour, use a plain chocolate with at least 70% chocolate solids (page 5).

300 g (11 oz) plain chocolate
150 g (5 oz) unsalted butter
6 eggs, separated
50 g (2 oz) caster sugar
2 teaspoons ground cinnamon

1   In a bowl over a pan of simmering water, melt the chocolate and the butter together.
2   Beat the egg yolks and 25 g (1 oz) sugar for about 1 minute, and then beat in the cinnamon.
3   With the chocolate and butter mixture still over the pan of water, stir in the egg yolk mixture and mix together thoroughly. Then remove the bowl from the heat.
4   In a clean, grease-free bowl, whisk the egg whites until they are very stiff. Beat the remaining sugar into the egg whites.
5   Gradually fold the egg whites into the chocolate mixture.
6   Spoon the mixture into a greased and lined 20 cm (8-inch) round cake tin.
7   Bake at Gas Mark 4/electric oven 180°C/fan oven 160°C for 30–40 minutes until the cake is dark golden in colour, well risen and springy to the touch.
8   Having removed the cake tin from the oven, place a sheet of foil over the top and allow to cool. This ensures that the steam from the cake produces a soft crust. Don't worry when the cake sinks, this is normal. Leave it in the tin to cool for 10 minutes before transferring it onto a wire rack to cool completely, unless you decide to eat it warm, which is also delicious.

MAKES 12
PREPARATION TIME: 10–15 minutes
COOKING TIME: 8–12 minutes

BRANDY SNAPS

These crisp biscuits, which are a long-time favourite, are flavoured with lemon zest and ginger. This is the traditional recipe when the brandy snaps are filled with whipped cream; they can also be served with ice cream. If you want to make baskets out of the brandy-snap mixture, mould the mixture around the bases of greased teacups.

50 g (2 oz) butter
50 g (2 oz) caster sugar
2 tablespoons golden syrup
50 g (2 oz) plain flour, sieved
1/2 teaspoon ground ginger
1 teaspoon brandy
grated zest of 1/2 unwaxed lemon
150 ml (5 fl oz) double cream

1   Melt the butter, sugar and syrup in a small saucepan over a gentle heat. Remove from the heat, stir in the remaining ingredients and mix well.
2   Place small teaspoonfuls of the mixture on greased and lined baking trays, remembering to allow room for spreading. It is probably better to place only 4 on each baking tray and to cook one tray at a time so you are able to shape them whilst they are still hot.
3   Bake at Gas Mark 4/electric oven 180°C/fan oven 160°C for 8–12 minutes, until puffy in texture and golden in colour.
4   Remove the tray from the oven and leave to cool and set for 1 minute. Loosen the brandy snaps with a palette knife and carefully roll twice around greased handles of wooden spoons, to form cylindrical shapes.
5   Leave the brandy snaps to set for about 5 minutes and then gently twist to remove them from the handles of the wooden spoons. Leave to cool and crisp on a wire rack.
6   Whip the cream until it is stiff, and then carefully fill the brandy snaps.

MAKES 30–40 bars
PREPARATION TIME: 20–25 minutes
COOKING TIME: 25–35 minutes

ENERGY BARS

The wonderful mix of ingredients in these bars makes them just right for that much-needed energy boost.

175 g (6 oz) unsalted butter
175 ml (6 fl oz) set honey
225 g (8 oz) demerara sugar
350 g (12 oz) rolled oats
1¹/₂ teaspoons ground cinnamon
115 g (4 oz) walnut pieces, chopped roughly
150 g (5 oz) raisins
15 g (5 oz) ready-to-eat dried apricots, chopped roughly
50 g (2 oz) pumpkin seeds
50 g (2 oz) sunflower seeds
50 g (2 oz) sesame seeds
50 g (2 oz) desiccated coconut

1   Melt the butter, honey and sugar in a large saucepan over a gentle heat. Cook for 5 minutes, stirring continuously. Bring to the boil and cook for 2 minutes until it resembles a smooth, thick sauce.
2   Combine all remaining ingredients together, mixing well. Stir them into the saucepan and mix thoroughly.
3   Divide the mixture between two greased and base-lined 30 x 19 cm (12- x 7¹/₂-inch) tins.
4   Bake at Gas Mark 5/electric oven 190°C/fan oven 170°C for 25–35 minutes until golden in colour and firm to the touch.
5   When cooked, remove the tins from the oven, loosen the edges with a knife and leave for 10 minutes.
6   Mark and cut into bars. Then place these onto a wire rack to cool completely.
7   When cold wrap each bar individually in greaseproof paper to store.

MAKES 12–16 slices
PREPARATION TIME: 45 minutes
COOKING TIME: 1¹/₄–1¹/₂ hours

FRUITY CAKE

This moist, buttery cake, which is made with a mixture of dates, prunes and dried apricots, tastes even better if left wrapped in foil for a couple of days before eating.

175 g (6 oz) butter
450 g (1 lb) mixed ready-to-eat dates, prunes, dried apricots, chopped
175 g (6 oz) dark muscovado sugar
100 ml (3¹/₂ fl oz) sweet sherry
100 ml (3¹/₂ fl oz) dark rum
1 teaspoon bicarbonate of soda
2 eggs, beaten
sieve together: 275 g (10 oz) plain flour
   ***and* 2 teaspoons ground mixed spice**
25 g (1 oz) flaked almonds

1   Place the butter, chopped fruits, sugar and alcohol in a large saucepan. Bring to the boil, stirring continuously. Reduce the heat to a to a gentle simmer for 15 minutes. Then allow to cool for 10 minutes.
2   Stir in the bicarbonate of soda. Don't be alarmed when the mixture froths up, which it is meant to do.
3   Stir in the eggs and fold in the flour and spice. Mix well to ensure an even texture.
4   Spoon the mixture into a greased and lined 20 cm (8-inch) round cake tin; smooth the top and sprinkle over the flaked almonds.
5   Bake at Gas Mark 2/electric oven 150°C/fan oven 130°F for 1¹/₂–1¹/₂ hours until dark golden in colour and a skewer inserted in the centre of cake comes out clean.
6   Cool the cake in the tin for 30 minutes. Then turn out on to a wire rack to cool completely.
7   Wrap the cake in foil and store for at least 2 days before serving.

ANZAC BISCUITS *pictured opposite*

MAKES approximately 20
PREPARATION TIME: 15 minutes
COOKING TIME: 20–25 minutes

115 g (4 oz) plain flour, sieved
115 g (4 oz) caster sugar
80 g (3 oz) rolled oats
80 g (3 oz) desiccated coconut
115 g (4 oz) butter
2 tablespoons golden syrup
I teaspoon bicarbonate of soda
2 tablespoons boiling water

These biscuits were made to be sent to the Anzacs – soldiers in the Australian and New Zealand Army Corps – when they were serving in Gallipoli during the First World War.

1 In a bowl, mix together the flour, caster sugar, oats and coconut.
2 Melt the butter and golden syrup together in a small saucepan.
3 Dissolve the bicarbonate of soda in the boiling water, and then stir it into the melted butter.
4 Pour the melted mixture into the dry ingredients, stirring well to combine.
5 Place dessertspoonfuls of the mixture onto greased baking sheets; remember to allow room for spreading.
6 Bake at Gas Mark 4/electric oven 180°C/fan oven 160°C for 20–25 minutes until golden.
7 Transfer the biscuits to a wire rack to cool.

OATCAKES

MAKES 15 bars
PREPARATION TIME: 10 minutes
COOKING TIME: 20–25 minutes

175 g (6 oz) medium oatmeal
115 g (4 oz) self-raising flour, sieved
½ teaspoon salt
25 g (1 oz) caster sugar
175 g (6 oz) butter
2 tablespoons water

These are an unleavened form of bread usually found in the north of England and Scotland They are traditionally eaten with cheese. Oatcakes can be round, triangular or bar shaped.

1 In a large bowl, place the oatmeal, flour, salt and sugar. Mix well together.
2 Melt the butter and water together, stir into the dry ingredients and mix to a firm dough.
3 Knead the dough gently. Then press into a lightly greased 33 x 23 cm (13- x 9-inch) Swiss roll tin.
4 Bake at Gas Mark 4/electric oven 180°C/fan oven 160°C for 20–25 minutes until pale golden in colour and firm to the touch.
5 Remove the tin from the oven and leave to cool for 5 minutes. Then mark and cut into 15 bars. Place the bars on a wire rack to cool completely.

MAKES approximately 20
PREPARATION TIME: 10 minutes
COOKING TIME: 12–15 minutes

MAKES 20–25 squares
PREPARATION TIME: 20 minutes
COOKING TIME: 1–1½ hours

GINGER BALLS

GINGERBREAD

These unusual cookies are crunchy outside and have a soft middle. For a variation, add 25 g (1 oz) of finely chopped stem ginger.

175 g (6 oz) self-raising flour, sieved
80 g (3 oz) soft light brown sugar
2 tablespoons ground ginger
½ teaspoon bicarbonate of soda
50 g (2 oz) margarine
3 tablespoons golden syrup
1 egg

1 In a bowl, mix together the flour, sugar, ginger and bicarbonate of soda.
2 In a medium-sized saucepan, melt the margarine and golden syrup over a gentle heat. Remove from the heat and allow to cool slightly.
3 Mix the melted mixture into the dry ingredients, together with the egg to form a stiff mixture.
4 Divide the cookie mixture into 20 pieces, shaped into balls.
5 Place the balls on lightly greased baking sheets, remembering to leave space between each.
6 Bake at Gas Mark 4/electric oven 180°C/fan oven 160°C for 12–15 minutes until golden in colour and puffy and firm to the touch.
7 When cooked remove from the oven, leave to cool on trays for 5 minutes. Then place the balls on a wire rack to cool completely.

This moist cake, containing ginger and black treacle, is very popular. It develops a deliciously sticky top if it is stored for a couple of days before being eaten. It is usually served cut into squares.

225 g (8 oz) butter, chilled
225 g (8 oz) dark brown soft sugar
16 tablespoons black treacle
2 eggs
sieve together: 350 g (12 oz) plain flour
** *and* 1 tablespoon ground ginger**
** *and* 2 teaspoons ground cinnamon**
1 teaspoon bicarbonate of soda
300 ml (½ pint) milk, warmed

1 In a large saucepan place the butter, sugar and black treacle and melt over a gentle heat until melted together. Allow to stand for 5 minutes.
2 Stir in the eggs and then mix in the flour and spices, ensuring everything is thoroughly mixed.
3 Dissolve the bicarbonate of soda in the milk; then gradually stir this into the melted mixture until well blended. The mixture will be very liquid.
4 Pour the mixture into a greased and lined 25cm (10-inch) square cake tin.
5 Bake at Gas Mark 1/electric oven 140°C/fan oven 120°C for 1–1½ hours until dark golden in colour, set and firm to the touch.
6 Remove the cake from the oven and leave it in the tin to cool for 15 minutes before placing it on a wire rack to cool completely.
7 This cake is best stored for 2–3 days, well wrapped in foil, before being eaten.

MAKES 12–16 slices
PREPARATION TIME: 20–25 minutes
COOKING TIME: 50–70 minutes

GINGER CAKE

There is a rich blend of flavours in this moist cake, which is best kept for two to three days before eating.

sieve together: 225 g (8 oz) plain flour
    and 1/2 teaspoon bicarbonate of soda
    and 1 teaspoon ground ginger
    and 1 teaspoon ground mixed spice
50 g (2 oz) medium oatmeal
12 tablespoons golden syrup
6 tablespoons black treacle
175 g (6 oz) butter
50 g (2 oz) molasses sugar
150 ml (5 fl oz) milk
115 g (4 oz) crystallized ginger, chopped finely
2 eggs

1. In a large bowl, mix the flour, bicarbonate of soda, ground ginger, mixed spice and the oatmeal.
2. In a saucepan, place the syrup, treacle, butter and sugar and milk and gently melt them over a medium heat. When melted, allow to cool for 5 minutes.
3. Stir the melted ingredients into the dry ingredients, together with the chopped ginger and the eggs; mix well.
4. Spoon the mixture into a greased and lined 20 cm (8-inch) round cake tin.
5. Bake at Gas Mark 4/electric oven 180°C/fan oven 160°C for 50–70 minutes until the cake is dark golden and firm to the touch.
6. Let the cake cool in the tin for 15 minutes. Then place it on a wire rack to cool completely.

MAKES 10–12 slices
PREPARATION TIME: 20 minutes
COOKING TIME: 20–30 minutes

RUM & GINGER CAKE

This dark, rich cake is ideal for an afternoon snack. Use the syrup from the jar of stem ginger for the topping.

50 g (2 oz) butter
80 g (3 oz) molasses sugar
8 tablespoons black treacle
1 egg
50 ml (2 fl oz) rum
115 g (4 oz) self-raising flour, sieved
2 teaspoons ground ginger
50 g (2 oz) stem ginger, sliced thinly

FOR THE TOPPING
50 g (2 oz) butter, softened
115 g (4 oz) icing sugar, sieved
3 tablespoons ginger syrup

1. In a saucepan, gently melt the butter, sugar and black treacle. Remove from the heat and allow to cool for 10 minutes.
2. Stir in the egg and rum, add the flour, ground ginger and ginger slices. Mix thoroughly.
3. Spoon the mixture into a greased and lined 20 cm (8-inch) sandwich cake tin, smooth the top.
4. Bake at Gas Mark 6/electric oven 200°C/fan oven 180°C for 20–30 minutes until the cake is dark golden in colour, set and firm to the touch.
5. Remove the cake from the oven and allow to cool in the tin for 10 minutes. Then transfer it onto a wire rack to cool completely.
6. To make the topping, beat all the ingredients together and spread it over the top of the cake.

BOILED FRUIT CAKE *pictured opposite*

MAKES 10–12 slices
PREPARATION TIME: 35 minutes
COOKING TIME: 1³⁄₄–2 hours

450 g (1 lb) mixed dried fruit
225 g (8 oz) caster sugar
115 g (4 oz) butter
1 teaspoon bicarbonate of soda
200 ml (7 fl oz) water
2 eggs
sieve together:
115 g (4 oz) wholemeal plain flour
and 115 g (4 oz) self-raising flour
and 1 tablespoon ground mixed spice
50 g (2 oz) glacé cherries, chopped

Combining the ingredients and then melting them together, produces a moist fruit cake which is **ideal for picnics**.

1 In a large saucepan, place the dried fruit, sugar, butter, bicarbonate of soda and water. Bring to the boil, and then simmer for 10 minutes. Allow to cool for 15 minutes.
2 Beat in the eggs, stir in the flours, spice and glacé cherries, mixing well.
3 Spoon the mixture into a greased and lined 18 cm (7-inch) round cake tin. Smooth the top.
4 Bake at Gas Mark 3/electric oven 160°C/fan oven 140°C for 1³⁄₄–2 hours until the cake is dark golden in colour, and a skewer inserted in the centre comes out clean.
5 Leave the cake in the tin for 15–20 minutes before placing it on a wire rack to cool completely.
6 Glaze the top of the cake with the warmed honey.

BARA BRITH

MAKES 10–12 slices
PREPARATION TIME: 30 minutes
COOKING TIME: 50–70 minutes

80 g (3 oz) currants
80 g (3 oz) sultanas
80 g (3 oz) butter, chilled
50 g (2 oz) candied peel
2 eggs, beaten
¹⁄₂ teaspoon ground mixed spice, sieved
80 g (3 oz) soft light brown sugar
350 g (12 oz) self-raising flour, sieved

TO GLAZE
2 tablespoons honey, warmed

This is a cake made which a mixture of dried fruits, and is especially **good for afternoon tea**. It can be served plain or buttered.

1 Place the currants and the sultanas in a saucepan, add 100 ml (3¹⁄₂ fl oz) water, simmer on a gentle heat for 15 minutes, drain well, and allow to cool for 15 minutes.
2 Put the cooled fruit into a bowl, mix in the butter and the peel. Beat in the eggs, spice and sugar. Fold in the flour and mix well.
3 Spoon the mixture into a greased and lined 900 g (2 lb) loaf tin. Smooth the top.
4 Bake at Gas Mark 2/electric oven 150°C/fan oven 130°F for 50–70 minutes, until the cake is dark golden in colour, and a skewer inserted in the centre comes out clean.
5 Allow the cake to cool in the tin for 15 minutes. Place it on a wire rack to cool completely.
6 Glaze with warmed honey.

This is the method used for preparing fatless sponges, Swiss rolls and Genoese sponges.

Traditionally, the eggs and sugar are whisked together for 10–15 minutes (depending on the type of whisk used) over hot water in order to dissolve the sugar completely and until the whisk leaves a trail when lifted out of the mixture. It is then whisked for a further 5 minutes off the heat while the mixture cools. A great deal of air is incorporated into the mixture at this stage, which gives the cake its light, spongy texture. Finally, the flour is folded in very carefully with a metal spoon so that the incorporated air is not lost.

THE WHISKING METHOD

If an electric mixer is used, the whisking time will be reduced and it will not be necessary to whisk over hot water.

The texture of a fatless sponge is even, light and very soft. It dries out extremely quickly and so should be eaten within 2 days of baking.

A Genoese sponge contains some fat but is made by the whisking method. The margarine is melted and trickled into the side of the mixture a little at a time and then folded in with the flour. This improves the flavour and the cake will keep longer than a fatless sponge.

PROBLEMS THAT CAN OCCUR WITH CAKES MADE BY THE WHISKING METHOD, AND REMEDIES

DOMED TOP
- Oven temperature too high: adjust temperature.
- Cake baked too high in oven: adjust shelf position.

TOO SHALLOW, NOT RISEN
- Insufficient whisking before adding flour: eggs and sugar should be at least double in bulk, and be able to hold the trail of the mixture.
- Too cool an oven: adjust temperature.
- Insufficient cooking: adjust cooking time.

CLOSE, DAMP TEXTURE
- Ingredients not measured properly: take care in measuring ingredients.
- Insufficient whisking before adding flour: eggs and sugar should be at least double in bulk, and be able to hold the trail of the mixture.
- Flour not folded in correctly: should be lightly folded in with a metal spoon.
- Oven too hot: adjust temperature
- Insufficient cooking: adjust cooking time

TOP WRINKLED AFTER BAKING
- Tin too small: use next size of tin.
- Slightly under-cooked, insufficient cooking: adjust cooking time.
- Flour not folded in correctly: should be lightly folded in with a metal spoon.
- Mixture spread unevenly in tin: ensure mixture is evenly spread.
- Cooking tin warped during cooking: buy a heavier gauge of tin.
- Oven shelves not level: adjust using a spirit level.

MAKES 16
PREPARATION TIME: 10 minutes
COOKING TIME: 25–30 minutes

ALMOND MACAROONS

These are delicious when served with a cup of tea or a glass of sweet wine.

2 egg whites
115 g (4 oz) ground almonds
175 g (6 oz) caster sugar
25 g (1 oz) ground rice
almond essence
16 blanched almonds
rice paper
icing sugar, to dust

1 Reserve 2 teaspoons of egg white. Place the remaining egg white in a clean, grease-free bowl. Whisk until soft peaks are formed.
2 Fold in the ground almonds, caster sugar, ground rice and a few drops of almond essence.
3 Line baking sheets with rice paper, place heaped teaspoonfuls of the mixture on the rice paper, remembering to leave space for the mixture to spread.
4 Brush the mounds with the reserved egg white and push a blanched almond into each.
5 Bake at Gas Mark 2/electric oven 150°C/fan oven 130°F for 25–30 minutes until the macaroons are pale golden in colour and firm to the touch.
6 Remove the macaroons from the oven and allow to cool for 5 minutes before transferring them onto a wire rack to cool completely. Carefully tear off the excess rice paper. Dust with icing sugar.

MAKES 10–12 slices
PREPARATION TIME: 30 minutes
COOKING TIME: 40–55 minutes

CHOCOLATE BROWNIE LOAF

This is a moist chocolate loaf with a brownie-type texture. Use chocolate with 70% cocoa solids (page 6) to give an intense flavour

150 g (5 oz) butter
50 g (2 oz) plain chocolate
200 g (7 oz) molasses sugar
2 eggs
vanilla essence
sieve together: 50 g (2 oz) plain flour
    and 1 teaspoon baking powder
150 g (5 oz) milk chocolate, chopped roughly

1 Place the butter and the dark chocolate in a bowl; melt over a pan of simmering hot water.
2 Put the sugar, eggs and a few drops of vanilla essence in a bowl. Beat them together until foamy, then stir in the flour and baking powder.
3 Stir in the melted butter and chocolate mixture. Fold in the milk chocolate.
4 Spoon the mixture into a greased and lined 900 g (2 lb) loaf tin; smooth the top.
5 Bake at Gas Mark 4/electric oven 180°C/fan oven 160°C for 40–55 minutes until the cake is firm and set.
6 Remove the cake from the oven and leave it in the tin for 10 minutes before placing it on wire rack to cool completely.

MAKES 8–12 slices
PREPARATION TIME: 15–20 minutes
COOKING TIME: 15–20 minutes

GENOESE CAKE

This light, moist sponge cake is made with a whisked egg mixture enriched with melted butter. This gives the sponge a rich and buttery taste. It will keep for 2–3 days.

3 eggs
115 g (4 oz) caster sugar
sieve together: 80 g (3 oz) plain flour
    and **1 tablespoon cornflour**
40 g (1½ oz) butter, melted and allowed to cool

FOR THE FILLING
4 tablespoons raspberry jam, warmed

1. Put the eggs and sugar in a deep bowl and whisk together until the mixture is thick enough to retain a trail of the whisk.
2. Fold half the flour and cornflour into the mixture very carefully; then repeat with the other half. Gently run in the butter at the edge of the bowl and fold in very lightly so the butter does not sink to the bottom, which would produce a heavy cake.
3. Spoon the mixture evenly between two 18 cm (7-inch) sandwich tins which have been greased and dusted with a mixture of flour and caster sugar. Tilt the mixture in the tins to spread evenly.
4. Bake at Gas Mark 5/electric oven 190°C/fan oven 170°C for 20–25 minutes until pale golden in colour and springy to the touch.
5. Remove the cakes from the oven and allow to cool in the tins for 5 minutes. Turn out onto a wire rack to cool completely.
6. When cold, sandwich the two halves together with jam and dust the top with caster sugar to serve.

MAKES 12–16 slices
PREPARATION TIME: 30 minutes soaking time + 15 minutes
COOKING TIME: 1½–2 hours

APRICOT, POLENTA & RICOTTA CAKE

This Italian cake, which has a sand-like, moist texture, is flavoured with almond and apricots. Polenta is a coarse, golden flour and ricotta is a fragrant Italian cheese with a delicate, smooth flavour, made from ewe's milk whey left over after other cheeses have been produced.

175 g (6 oz) ready-to-eat dried apricots, chopped coarsely
3 tablespoons amaretto liqueur
sieve together: 115 g (4 oz) self-raising flour
    and **115 g (4 oz) self-raising wholemeal flour**
    and **1 teaspoon baking powder**
    and **1 tablespoon ground cinnamon**
175 g (6 oz) polenta
225 g (8 oz) caster sugar
250 g (9 oz) ricotta cheese
115 g (4 oz) butter, melted
200 ml (7 fl oz) warm water
80 g (3 oz) walnut pieces, chopped

1. Place the apricots in a bowl, add the liqueur and allow to soak for at least 30 minutes.
2. In a large bowl, place the flours, baking powder, ground cinnamon, polenta and sugar.
3. In another bowl, whisk together the ricotta cheese, melted butter and water. Then whisk this into the flour mixture until well blended.
4. Stir in the apricots, any remaining liqueur and the chopped nuts.
5. Spoon the mixture into a greased and lined 20 cm (8-inch) round cake tin.
6. Bake at Gas Mark 3/electric oven 170°C/fan oven 150°C for 1½–2 hours until the cake is pale golden in colour and a skewer inserted into the centre of the cake comes out clean.
7. Remove the cake from the oven and leave to cool in the tin for 30 minutes before placing it on a wire rack to cool completely.

MAKES 8–12 slices
PREPARATION TIME: 15–20 minutes
COOKING TIME: 15–20 minutes

This is a light, fatless cake usually filled with jam but, for a special occasion, it is delicious filled with whipped double cream as well.

3 eggs
115 g (4 oz) caster sugar
75 g (3 oz) plain flour, sieved

FOR THE FILLING
4 tablespoons raspberry jam

SERVES 8–12 slices
PREPARATION TIME: 15–20 minutes
COOKING TIME: 10–20 minutes

This long-time favourite is a light sponge cake made in a large shallow rectangular tin, then spread with jam and rolled up. To make a chocolate Swiss roll, replace 25 g (1 oz) of flour with cocoa powder. Warming the jam will help it spread more easily.

3 eggs
75 g (3 oz) caster sugar
75 g (3 oz) plain flour, sieved
1 tablespoon hot water

FOR THE FILLING
6 tablespoons raspberry jam, warmed

BASIC SPONGE CAKE

1 Put the eggs and sugar in a deep bowl and whisk together until the mixture is thick enough to retain a trail of the whisk.
2 Fold half the flour into the mixture very carefully; repeat with remaining flour
3 Spoon the mixture evenly between two 18 cm (7-inch) sandwich tins, which have been greased and dusted with a mixture of flour and caster sugar. Tilt the mixture in the tins to spread evenly.
4 Bake at Gas Mark 5/electric oven 190°C/fan oven 170°C for 15–20 minutes until pale golden in colour and springy to the touch.
5 Remove cakes from oven and allow to cool in the tins for 5 minutes. Turn out onto a wire rack to cool completely.
6 When cold, sandwich the two halves together with jam and dust top with caster sugar to serve.

SWISS ROLL

1 Put the eggs and sugar in a deep bowl and whisk together until the mixture is thick enough to retain a trail of the whisk.
2 Fold half the flour into the mixture very carefully repeat with the remaining flour. Lightly stir in the water.
3 Spoon the mixture into a greased and lined 33 x 23 cm (13- x 9-inch) Swiss roll tin, tilting the tin to ensure the mixture is spread evenly.
4 Bake at Gas Mark 7/electric oven 220°C/fan oven 200°C for 10–20 minutes until it is golden-brown in colour and springy to the touch.
5 Have ready a sheet of greaseproof paper liberally sprinkled with caster sugar. Turn the cooked sponge onto the paper, then remove the paper which had been lining the base of the tin. Trim the edges of the sponge and spread the surface with warmed jam.
6 Roll up the sponge, making the first roll firmly which will give the finished cake a good shape.
7 Dredge the cake with caster sugar, and set onto a wire rack to cool completely.

VARIATION
Should you wish to fill a Swiss roll with whipped double cream, roll up the cooked cake with greaseproof paper in the centre and allow the cake to cool completely. Carefully unroll and fill with cream and jam and then re-roll, sprinkle with caster sugar and serve immediately.

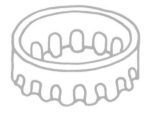

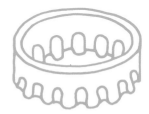

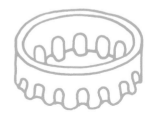

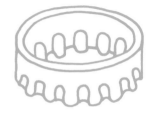